DISPLACED BUT NOT LOST

War Through the Eyes of a Child

TONY M. TAAGEN

ISBN-10: 147503220X
ISBN-13: 9781475032208
Library of Congress Control Number: 2012909451
CreateSpace Independent Publishing Platform
North Charleston, South Carolina

COMMENTS BY A SON, ON THE BOOK BY THE FATHER

I consider this book one of the best that I have read. Although it is a work of nonfiction, I rank it with such great 20th century novelists as Twain, Steinbeck, Hemingway, and Remarque.

Surprisingly for a memoir, it flows like a novel, and it is a true classic in the sense that the messages it conveys are timeless. While dealing with WW2 specifically, it is actually about any war (or any situation of desperation and survival).

Some of the short chapters can stand alone like poetry, in the style of Bukowski, and the longer chapters can stand alone as novellas.

The audience for this book has a broad range, from scholars such as ethnographers and historians, to those just seeking an entertaining and adventurous read. The photos alone are a treasure, dating from a period and place where most photos were lost to war.

This memoir is a unique mix of history, culture, philosophy, humor, and reflection. *Told Through the Eyes of a Child*, is a reminder of the wisdom of children. A reminder that kids are astute, and capable of observing, analyzing, and reacting—especially under conditions of survival and deprivation.

As one of the sons of the author, I grew up influenced by many of the stories included here. They have definitely given me a more analytical and nuanced view of the daily world news, and yes, perhaps a jaundiced view. In that vein, please note the book's subtitle, *War Through The Eyes of a Child* and recognize that it is truly written from this perspective, even down to the vernacular of a child. Yes, there are some stories that are not included because my father was protected from them until later, or never told them directly. Furthermore, I think most authors would recognize that only fiction can portray the truths that true stories must omit, to protect the participants and heirs from embarrassment, mistakes, and misinterpretation that can accompany all legacies.

One modern day message of the book is that it exhibits how the daily shift and flow of a particular war is more than a newspaper headline to the innocent bystanders on the ground. It has been about 150 years since the Civil War. That is the last time the United States has seen true combat on its homeland. The wars we currently support and export are short-lived, indeed, in our memories. It is easy to forget that a few short years of direct war easily consumes 15 to 20 years if one includes pre and post war turmoil for the victims—encompassing a lost childhood for the young, and a lost adulthood for the mature.

In conclusion, just a couple of story updates from a son and grandson. My grandfather, Johannes, eventually gave up trying to turn Tony into a banker, and started encouraging and correcting my math homework. I was more naive than my father and incapable of even considering avoidance, and eventually I became an engineer—the best in all my Math classes at Marquette University, Milwaukee, Wisconsin (not that it has done me any good in my current position as an acrobat in a band).

I think that my father was influenced in a good way by the war. His two most outstanding characteristics are his apathy to the daily drama of life that can consume many lives, and his empathy for those trapped in their own efforts to survive. He knows what is truly important. Everyone has something they devote their lives to, be it business, art, sport, or some other endeavor/obsession. Tony has spent his life putting others first, and using his survival skills to teach or help others to survive. For instance, volunteering social services to the poor, yes, even at times acting as their banker and advisor. For my five brothers and me, Tony has always been ready to drop everything after getting that phone call from the authorities or the hospital, and to drive for hours, if necessary, to get us out of a jam. Two years in a row he told me that my trip down the Mississippi River might not be a good idea, but he still helped me to launch—and both years he got that nighttime phone call to come get me after I sank the boat. He is good in a crisis, a good survivor, and always looks first to the mental and physical comfort of others.

Enjoy the memoir; it is a true story of adventure, if one defines an adventure as a tragedy which one survives, hopefully to never repeat, yet enriched by wisdom gained and empathy felt for others.

Tom Taagen

“IF THE FIRST BUTTERFLY YOU SEE IN THE SPRING IS BLACK, YOU WILL DIE BEFORE THE YEAR IS OUT.”

Mari Kallion Tagen, author’s paternal grandmother

For my wife, Constance Ann Kelley Taagen, and our six sons: Thomas John, Matthew Kelley, Timothy Tyler, Sam Rand, Julian Constant, and Jess Last. Because of your curiosity, I have written this true story of my early life, so different from your own.

◎ TAAGEN (TAGEN) FAMILY TREE

TMT

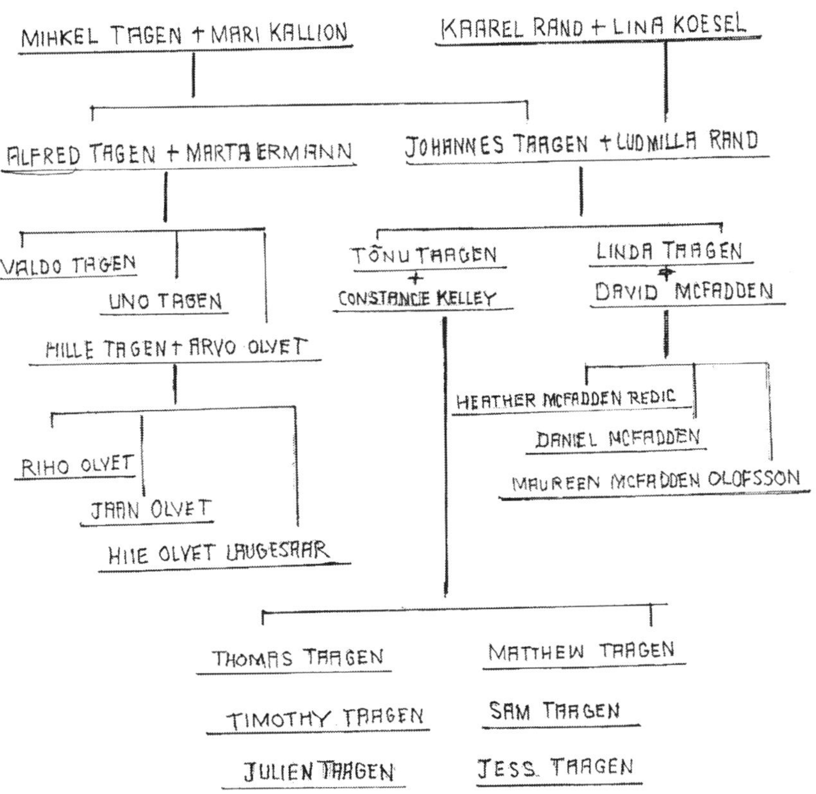

◎ Johannes Taagen added an extra "a" to Tagen (approx. 1934) to sound more Estonian.

1. Estonian places mentioned in the book T.M.T.

2. ROUTE of the MOLTKEFELS

T.M.T.

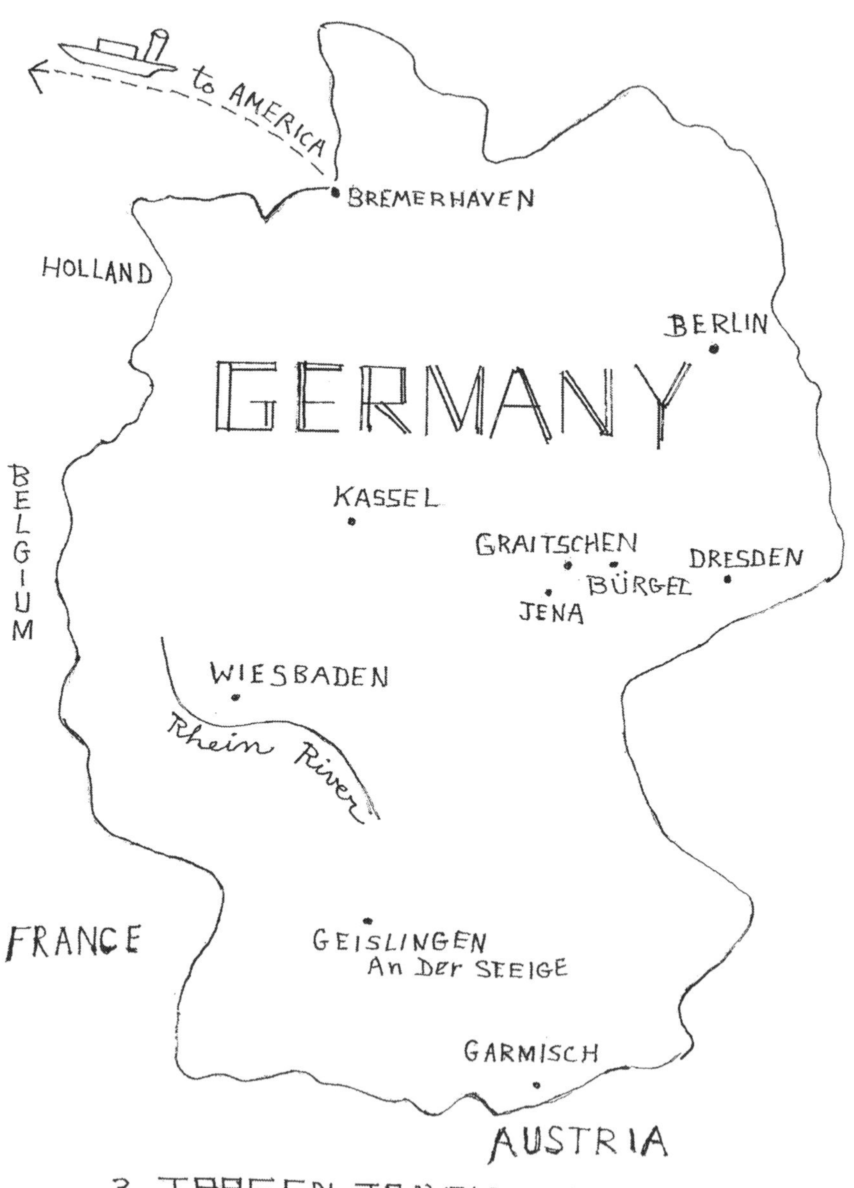

3. TRAGEN TRAVELS IN GERMANY
1944-1949

T.M.T.

Photo List

1. Author arriving in homeland, Tallinn, Estonia, September 9, 1999.
2. Author arriving in homeland, Tallinn, Estonia, Sept. 9, 1999, with sister and others.
3. Tallinn Harbor with relatives, September 9, 1999.
4. Cemetery visit.
5. Author reunited with cousin, Hille Tagen Olvet, his closest living relative in Estonia.
6. Bank building, Tallinn Street, Viljandi.
7. Gateway to castle built by Teutonic Knights, 1200s, Viljandi.
8. Barn at Tuule (Wind) Farm.
9. Old Walled City, Tallinn.
10. Old Town Square, Tallinn.
11. Old Town Square, Tallinn. Author and Hiie Olvet Laugesaar.
12. Paternal grandparents with sons, Alfred and Johannes. Johannes is wearing his Tartu University cap.
13. Fraternity gathering, winter, 1936, Viljandi. Johannes is kissing woman in back row. Ludmilla is in front row, third from right.
14. Author's parents with maternal grandfather. Assumed to be before 1934. Couple on left is unidentified.
15. Author's baptism, 1934.
16. Author with mother, 1934.
17. Seaside resort, Pärnu, 1935. Author on mother's lap. Author's father on right.

36. Author, back row between mother and father, and other Estonian passengers on the Marine Tiger.

37. Author on board Marine Tiger wearing fur cap.

38. Arrival in New York, February 27, 1949. Family and Mr. Cozby in front of unnamed hotel.

39. Arrival in Texas, March 2, 1949.

40. Housewarming, Springtown, Texas.

41. Housewarming newspaper article and photo of mother and sponsor, Jessie Cozby.

42. Author driving tractor, summer, 1949.

43. Donations to Taagen family from friends and neighbors.

44. Author, high school, West Bend, Wisconsin.

Photos courtesy of Ludmilla Rand Taagen, Tony M. Taagen, Hiie Olvet Laugesaar, and Jaan Tuuksma. Number 41, permission granted by Fort Worth Star-Telegram, Texas. Number 44, photo by West Bend Daily News, permission granted by Daily News, West Bend, Wisconsin.

CONTENTS

Chapter 1.

RETURNING HOME TO ESTONIA *(EESTI)*, SEPTEMBER, 1999

I am sitting at an outside table. A small restaurant, in Stockholm Harbor. I keep drinking coffee. I'm on my fifth cup. The waitress refuses a tip. She says, "It is not necessary." I insist that she keep the money.

Connie, my wife; Tom, our oldest son; Linda, my sister; and her husband, David, are nearby. Only another two hours before the Baltic Kristina sails for Tallinn, Estonia, my homeland and my sister's. It is a fourteen-hour cruise. People are boarding.

Finally, we board. The ship takes off; we pass many small islands in the Swedish archipelago. I see two Swedish gunboats heading toward land. They blend into the sea, barely visible.

Suddenly, my mind transports me to the freighter Moltkefels, in August, 1944, moored in Tallinn Harbor. My mother is here. So are my sister and father. He cannot leave. He must remain to defend the country. We are saying good-bye. Everyone is crying. He departs, and the ship sails for Danzig, Germany, by way of Riga, Latvia. We have dried bread and lard, prepared by my mother weeks before, in case there is no food on board. I am ten years old and aware of the seriousness of our situation. But I try to see it as an adventure. I am hopeful things will be better.

The Kristina, in September, 1999, is luxurious, with several bars, cocktail lounges, restaurants, casino, and dance floors. To me, our cabin is beautiful. Connie, my wife, feels closed in.

I think again of the Moltkefels in August, 1944, sleeping on a flat surface, enclosed by low boards. No pillow and only a grey woolen blanket my mother brought along from Tuule farm. I'm a little seasick but possess the curiosity of a ten-year-old boy.

But now, I remind myself, I'm standing on the deck of the Kristina. Not the Moltkefels.

However, I am vividly recalling the bomber overhead as we were transported by the Moltkefels. The bomber is Russian. The antiaircraft guns are beginning to fire. I am told that the plane has dropped a bomb. But it missed.

Now I go back inside the Kristina. It's another world. Things have changed. The band is playing. People are laughing. I am no longer on the Moltkefels. It is 1999, and I am speaking easily in Estonian. My fluency both surprises and pleases me.

Thus, we sail on through the Swedish archipelago, over the Baltic Sea, and into Tallinn Harbor, with the red roofs of the Old Town shining before us. My sister and I stand shoulder to shoulder at the rail. Remembering.

Gently, the Baltic Kristina nudges the Tallinn dock. The gangplank is lowered. I am home, at last. We hastily gather our belongings and are directed to customs, where our luggage is examined, our passports are stamped, and my nervousness mounts along with anticipation. Will anyone be here to greet us? Will I recognize anyone? When we left in 1944, I was ten years old and Linda was seven.

I observe a group of people who are waving to us. I take a deep breath of Estonian air. This is it! Immediately, I see my cousin Hille's daughter Hiie, whom we met when she visited us in Brown Deer, Wisconsin, in 1992, one year after Estonian Reindependence on August 20, 1991. My sister and her husband had sent Hiie funds for a ticket, and after much red tape, she came— a daring teenager— to represent the family. Young, scared, able to speak only halting English, but exceedingly brave to come so far alone after years of Soviet repression, she possessed the determination and sense of fun of teenagers everywhere. Now seven years later, she is grown-up and married and, fortunately for us, looks the same.

As we quickly approach the group of relatives, I reflect that I have achieved something that I never really expected to see happen. A dream has come true. But I am determined to maintain my composure.

We all rush toward one another, and everyone is hugging, shaking hands, and introducing themselves at once in Estonian and halting English or English and halting Estonian amidst more hugging, laughter, and mounting exuberance.

Briefly, I am saddened because my parents did not have the opportunity to experience this wondrous homecoming, which they deserved more than my sister and I deserve it. But with this overwhelming welcome, sadness fades and I am overjoyed in the moment. I glance at Linda and see tears in her eyes, but they disappear and are replaced by a smile. I realize they were tears of joy. We are home.

Eventually, someone takes charge, and we are bustled into cars by these remaining Estonian relatives who have come to Tallinn to welcome us. We are swiftly on our way to Viljandi, my sister's and my hometown. We stop along the way, more than once, to visit the family graves, as is the custom. We place flowers and candles on the well-tended graves in their park-like settings. Wrought iron fences surround each family plot, and we tidy the ground with a nearby rake as we remember each beloved relative.

When we arrive in Viljandi, we visit the ruins of the old castle behind our childhood home. It is where we played in the summer and sledded in the winter, ever mindful that a virgin was believed to have been entombed in the castle wall, for good luck, sometime in the thirteenth century. We thought, as children, that we could see the wall of the tomb glowing at night, and we always ran away in great fright. And secret delight.

Next, we walk past our father's bank at Number 3 Tallinn Street. We are pleasantly surprised that the building is still here. We marvel at how it looks the same. I look for the second floor, and abruptly my mind transports me to the winter of 1942, the German occupation, and the vision of snow-white naked bodies fills my being. I control my thoughts and realize it is now September 1999, warm and peaceful.

We walk to Turu Street where we lived. Our house seems to be gone. I walk down the alley. Isn't there anything left? The outdoor market is familiar. I walk past a grey building on an adjoining street. Suddenly, I remember scenes from the autumn of 1940 and the Russian occupation; Russian voices coming from the basement of that grey building, and screams. I push the nightmare away. I remind myself it is September 1999, warm and peaceful.

My relatives suggest we visit nearby Tuule Farm, home of our paternal grandparents, where I spent so many happy summers surrounded by love and sheep. Upon our arrival, I expect my grandmother to come rushing out of the house to embrace us and my grandfather to stride from the stone barn to offer us a cup of his birch bark brew. Instead, we are greeted by the current owners, a Russian woman and her son, who could not have known this spot in August 1944.

But I remember. How can I not? I was too young for military service, but old enough to remember; eventually displaced, but not lost—remembering always—war through the eyes of a child.

Chapter 2.

1939: VILJANDI

My father, Johannes, goes to work every day. He is the president of the bank. My mother Ludmilla, and the maid stay home. My mother takes me, Tõnu, and my sister Linda, with her when she goes to the cafe where she always meets her friends. Now it is forenoon at the cafe. I am five years old, and I am bored. My sister behaves because she is only two. I create a disturbance by wandering off. My mother seems upset and tells me that, from now on, I have to stay at home when she goes to meet her friends.

A few days later, she tells me to go to my room and stay until she returns. She tells me that I cannot go along, because I have misbehaved. She takes me to the maid's room. As she leaves, she locks the door, and I am alone. I hear her footsteps leaving the house, and as I go to the window, I see her leave the yard.

I suddenly realize that a fire is burning in the stove. I open the door of the stove, and I stare into the fire. I start throwing things into the flames—pieces of paper, chopped pieces of wood that are piled up near the stove. The flames roar, and I manage to close the door to the stove.

After a while, I hear my mother return. She unlocks the door, and I pretend to be asleep. As she touches me I open my eyes, and she tells me that, if I behave in the future, she will take me to the cafe. I pretend not to hear her, and I leave the room. I am five years old.

Chapter 3.

MY FIRST DRINK OF WINE, 1939

I am still five years old, and my mother is having a dinner party. It is a long table, and the maid is serving the food. I am sent outside to play with Linda, but we get cold and sneak back into the house and hide in another part of the house.

I hear laughter in the living room and sneak into the dining room. My sister follows me. I see the maid taking away dishes and food. She leaves the room, and I move closer to the table where I see many glasses. The glasses have traces of a red liquid in them. I start drinking the unfinished drinks, one by one, as I make my way around the table. The liquid is bitter, but I continue drinking. Linda does not drink any. She is only two years old.

Suddenly, the maid enters—and I run from the room. I go to my bedroom and sit on my bed. The bitter taste is gone from my mouth, and I feel dizzy— but good. I have discovered a drink that I like.

Chapter 4.

A NIGHTMARE RETURNS

It is now the fall of 1940. I am six years old, and it is the Russian occupation. One dark afternoon, the adults speak in whispers about the Russians coming and they have no time for my questions, so I walk outside to the high wooden fence in front of our house and look out through a crack in the boards. The market square before me is filled with Russian trucks. Not far from my hole in the fence I see a Russian soldier playing an accordion. Two of the soldiers are dancing. Spinning around with their arms locked at the elbow. They are all laughing. I see a soldier bending over a helmet filled with water. He is washing his face and drinking water out of his cupped hands and spitting it back into the helmet. I turn without thinking and run back to the house.

One day, I am walking home from school with two friends. As we walk past a grey building, screams come from a basement window. They are a man's screams. We sneak to the window, and it is open. We try to peek in, as we huddle around the opening. The screams get louder. Suddenly, we hear a shot. The screams become moans, and then there is silence. We hear men speaking in Russian. They laugh. We run. We know that someone is being tortured. We gather a distance away from the building. We wonder, do we know this man who screamed, and moaned? We are scared for the moment. But the fear leaves us soon, maybe because we are becoming used to horror, which is beginning to present itself with greater frequency since the Russians have come in.

Maybe it is because I am six years old. I tell no one. But I have nightmares about it for a long time.

Chapter 5.

JUNE 21, 1941: START OF WAR

We are visiting Piirita, a small town near Tallinn, on the Gulf of Finland. My mother and sister are here, and my father arrives later from his hiding place in Tallinn, where he has been living in a friend's attic since the Russians came in 1939.

Linda and I are not allowed to know where he is living because my mother says it is a secret. He went into hiding the day he went to work, in 1939, and an Estonian woman, who my mother said was a friend of the Russians, was sitting at his desk with a gun. She said to him, "I am in charge now, and if I knew what you are thinking, I would shoot you now."

I have only seen him during this time of Russian occupation when he has made short nighttime visits to the Tuule farm, where my grandparents live.

The house we are staying at, in Piirita, belongs to a friend of my parents, and there are several other visitors. It is a beautiful day, and I am happy.

Suddenly, the adults begin to listen to the radio. The mood changes; the adults whisper. There is no more laughter. The men gather shovels and start to dig a hole inside a shed. They work into the night. I ask my father why they are digging, and he tells me that the Germans have attacked Russia, and we have to be safe in case of an air raid. I am not fearful. My father is here.

Finally, the hole is finished, and the men fill the bottom with straw. The hole reminds me of a grave. Around midnight, there are planes in the air. We all run from the house, enter the shed, and climb down into the hole. Suddenly, a man begins to curse. Water is entering the hole.

We listen for the sound of the planes. They are gone. We all climb out of the hole and go back into the house.

My mother tells me to return to sleep in the corner of a small room. It is next to a room where the adults are talking. They open bottles of wine. Now there is laughter as they listen to the crackling sounds of the radio.

I hear the adults say that the Russians have been attacked by the Germans. It is June 21, 1941. I am seven years old. My sister is four years old. My mother is thirty-three years old. My father is thirty-six years old.

The following day, we leave. My parents seem to be in a hurry. There are planes overhead, but we don't know whose they are. We take a bus to Tallinn. On the way, the bus is stopped by Russian soldiers. They enter the bus and begin to examine the individual identity documents, which all adults are required to carry. I'm sitting next to my father, and my sister is sitting with my mother.

Two soldiers are examining the personal documents of each rider. I see my father paging through his document, which looks like a little book with his picture on the inside page. He quickly tears out a page and stuffs it into the side pocket of his jacket. One of the soldiers stops at our seat, and my father hands him the document. The soldier pages through it. And hands it back. The soldiers continue to the rear of the bus. There is some loud talking behind us, and the Russians escort a man off the bus. They motion to the driver to go. As the bus pulls out, a woman in the back of the bus begins to sob. I look out the window and see the man led to a truck. He looks back at the bus. The woman screams and then, again, begins to sob. I realize that the man's documents showed something was not in order.

The bus arrives in Tallinn, and we get off. As we walk down a street, I ask my father why he ripped a page out of the book. He says that he will tell me someday. As we walk on, my father enters a building through a back door. He does not say good-bye. He just leaves.

My mother, my sister, and I go to the train station and take a train to Viljandi. Our 160 kilometer ride to Viljandi takes forever because the train makes many stops, during which Russian soldiers board the train. Whenever that happens, I see men jump out of the open windows and disappear.

We arrive in Viljandi at nearly midnight, but it is not dark. I suddenly realize that it is almost the longest day of the year, *Jaanipaev*, or St. John's Day. However, there are no celebrations or bonfires or people singing and dancing. The only reminder of this time of year is that the daylight is endless. We go to bed and rise with the light.

After we arrive at our house, Number 11 Turu Street, I ask my mother why my father stayed in Tallinn. She tells me that the Russians are trying to find him. If they do, he will undoubtedly be sent to Siberia. She tells me to keep his location a secret and not to tell anyone, even if they ask. He is in hiding. I am seven years old, and my sister is four, and I tell her we can keep a secret.

Chapter 6.

KNOCK ON THE DOOR

My cousin Valdo arrives in the night. There are planes overhead, but no bombs. He is sixteen years old and tells us that he has been staying at the Tuule Farm with our grandparents. But since war began between Germany and Russia, he feels that it is not safe for him to be there—especially since his parents, my uncle Alfred and Aunt Marta, and his sister, my cousin Hille, were sent to Siberia by the Russians earlier in June. The day they were taken, Valdo was not at home, and his younger brother Uno was at a youth camp. He feels he can no longer take chances, or he, likewise, will be captured. I have spent lots of time with Valdo over the years. I know him well, and I don't want to see him leave. He tells me he will be staying with other relatives where he will be safe. He stays the night, then leaves quickly.

The next night, June 23, as we are about to go to bed, there is a loud knock on the front door. My mother, my sister, and I approach the door. I think that perhaps it is my father. As my mother unlocks the door, I see a woman I do not recognize. She is gesturing and talking in a whisper. She says, "Leave now; they are coming for you." Before my mother has a chance to talk, the woman disappears.

My mother quickly shuts the door, lifts my sister, and tells me to follow her. We run out the back door, carrying nothing, and continue running toward a large field near our house. Then we turn to the right and reach a small valley grown with trees.

It is still not dark, although, the hour is late. We start walking through the thicket, and after about ten minutes, we stop. My mother listens. It is quiet. She tells me that we have to go to the Tuule Farm, because Russians are looking for my father, and if they find us, they will take us, also. By now, I realize that being captured by the Russians means certain deportation to Siberia.

We circle the town by staying on small roads and paths. Eventually, we arrive at the road that will, after approximately fourteen kilometers, take us to the Tuule Farm. We avoid the main roads and walk through the forests lining the road. We stop to rest, and my sister is crying. My mother tells me to carry her. I do it for a while, then suddenly realize that I am getting very tired.

It is well beyond midnight, and we go on. I am getting hungry and thirsty. We walk on, but after a short distance, my mother tells me that we have to rest. We all lie down under a fir tree, and in no time, fall asleep.

I am awakened by my mother. The sun is coming up, and I am hungry and thirsty, but say nothing. She tells me that we have about two hours before we reach the Tuule Farm and my grandparents. We start walking, still staying off the road. We suddenly enter a small meadow, and I discover patches of wild strawberries. I drop to my knees and start picking the ripe berries. I eat them immediately. My mother does the same, but shares hers with my sister. The berries seem to satisfy my hunger and thirst. My mother tells me that we must go on. We walk on, my mother holding my sister's hand.

And suddenly, I see my grandparents' farm in the distance. As we leave the forest, we walk across a field and we are there. My grandparents come out of the house, and my mother speaks to them in a whisper.

We eat ham sandwiches and drink milk. I go out into the apple orchard, lie down, and fall asleep immediately. We have walked through the night and the forest for over fourteen kilometers.

Chapter 7.

MY MOTHER LEAVES THE FARM

When I awaken from my sleep, it's late afternoon. My mother tells me that she must go. She is leaving me and my sister with these grandparents, who are my father's parents, and also the grandparents of my cousins Valdo, Uno, and Hille.

They wonder where my cousin Valdo is now—and where Uno, his younger brother by four years, could be. Uno has not been seen in weeks. My grandmother hopes that these grandchildren will both return to Tuule Farm safely and soon. I overhear her tell my mother that they are very worried about the boys' parents and sister—somewhere in Siberia.

My grandfather is going to take my mother to Viljandi in the evening. I tell them all that I would like to go along, because they are taking a horse and a wagon. They tell me that I must stay to help my grandmother.

My mother dresses in old peasant clothing. She wears a long skirt, a large blouse, and a large scarf on her head. The scarf hides most of her face. She looks very old, and she explains that she does not want to be recognized. My grandmother gives her an old sack filled with ham pieces and a loaf of rye bread. My mother tells me to help my grandparents. She gives my sister a hug. They climb onto the wagon, and my grandfather slaps the reins. The horse moves, and they take off.

My sister and I run after the wagon as it disappears around a curve. My sister starts to cry, and I take her hand. My grandmother is suddenly behind us as we turn. She sinks to her knees, holds both of us in her arms, and says nothing. I know everything has changed since the men in Piirita were listening to the crackling of the radio.

But I am confused about everything—about my father in hiding, the woman at our door, the long walk through the forest, and now my mother leaving. Now, my grandmother tells me that everything will be all right. She says it will probably be a long time, but my parents will return.

We eat supper, but I am not hungry. She tells me that I will be helping with the cows and sheep. She also tells me that I will be sleeping above the stone barn. My sister will be in the farmhouse.

Chapter 8.

FIRST NIGHT AT TUULE FARM

My grandfather returns from taking my mother to Viljandi. He tells me that she is staying with friends. I wonder what happened in our house the night before, after we left, when the woman came to the door and whispered something. I think about the long walk to the farm, and the fact that my mother and father are not here. I wonder if I will ever see them again. It makes me sad.

My grandmother joins us as my grandfather is unhitching the horse from the wagon. We walk the horse into the barn yard, and my grandfather releases him.

My grandfather and I go to the benches in front of the house. He fills a tin cup with something he calls fermented birch bark brew and hands it to me. He tells me to taste, and I take a swallow. It's bitter. But I like it. He finishes the cup and places it on a hook on the barrel. My grandmother walks up to me and tells me that she is glad that I came. She tells me that I am almost an adult, and can help on the farm. She tells me that she and my grandfather would like me to take the twelve cows and thirty sheep into the pastures every morning, and watch them during the day. I will be accompanied by the large white dog that seems to follow me wherever I go. I tell her that I am looking forward to this task.

I pause to think about this duty. It arouses some fright in me, as I will be by myself, with the dog for company, spending the days in a pasture surrounded by a dark forest. My grandmother must sense what I'm thinking. She comes to me, puts her hand on my shoulder, and tells me that everything will be fine.

She tells me to go to sleep upstairs in the stone barn. She tells me that my sleeping area has been prepared. She walks me to the ladder which leans against the end of the barn and leads to the opening for the upstairs. I climb the ladder and turn. She tells me that I will be awakened at five in the morning. There are no windows upstairs in the stone barn, but I can see enough light through the opening where the ladder rests. I walk to the flax bag which is my bed. I take off my shoes and crawl into the bag without removing my clothes. I think about going to bed at our house in Viljandi. I had a bed with a mattress, covered with sheets, and a pillow. We also had electric lights and a bathroom. Here we have a well for water, an outside toilet, and candles and kerosene lanterns. This is much different.

Things have changed a lot in two days. My thoughts are interrupted by the barking of the big white dog beside the outside ladder at the end of the barn. I crawl out of my sack and walk softly to the opening. I look down and see the dog. I whistle. He looks up, makes a whining sound, and lies down. I walk back to my new bed, crawl into the sack, and quickly fall asleep, because I am still tired from our walk through the night.

Chapter 9.

FIRST DAY AS A SHEPHERD

I'm awakened by the cows making sounds, below me, in the barn. I get up, put on my shoes, and leave my new bedroom by climbing down the ladder. I walk to the house and find my grandparents in the kitchen, where my grandmother is preparing ham and eggs. We sit down and eat.

My grandmother leaves the kitchen and returns with a white shirt and white pants. She also places a pair of shoes on my lap, along with white long pieces of cloth. She tells me that I will wrap these pieces around my feet and continue wrapping them around my ankles and up my lower legs to below the knees. She helps me with the task. She picks up one of the shoes, which looks like a small narrow basket. It is made out of strips of willow bark tied together at the edges with long straps of leather. I place my wrapped foot into the willow bark, and she begins to wrap the leather straps around the strips of cloth. When the straps are below the knee, she ties a knot. We repeat the wrapping and tying with the other foot.

After this, I am told to change into the long shirt and pants. They are made out of flax which she has raised, spun into thread, and woven. The flax cloth feels comfortable. She tells me that she will put my own clothes away, and I will wear them when I again go to Viljandi.

I am given a cloth bag which has a strap and is filled with ham sandwiches. She also hands me a metal container with a cover. It is full of water.

My grandfather says he will help me lead the cows and sheep to the pasture, and explains to me the limits of the area within which I have to keep the animals that are now my responsibility. He releases the animals from the barn, and we head for the forest. I suddenly realize that the big white dog is following us. I ask my grandfather if the dog can stay with me, and he tells me that the dog will be with me. He also explains that the dog knows the boundaries of the pastures and says, if any of the animals stray beyond their limits, the dog will chase them back. I am comforted that the dog will be helping me.

We enter a path that goes through a dark forest filled with ferns. After what seems a long distance, we are in a meadow. My grandfather says that, when it is time to return, he will ring the bell near the barn. He places his hand on my shoulder, tells me to be brave, and leaves.

Suddenly, I am alone. I look around at the surrounding forest and try not to think about what lies beyond its edge and the darkness within. The big white dog seems to sense my concern, and rubs against my leg. I find a large birch tree near the border of the heavy firs and sit down with my back against the tree. I can see the cattle and the sheep. The big white dog lies down near me and falls asleep. I am relaxed and become very tired. I know that I cannot fall asleep. I try to think about the afternoon when I will round up the animals and return to the farm.

I decide to get up and walk around in my willow-bark shoes. They are comfortable. I walk to an old wooden structure across the meadow, with the dog following. The animals are lying down near the edge of the forest. I enter the log shed through a large opening in the front. As I look into the darkness, my eyes become accustomed to the light. I notice dirty rags and a large flax sheet spread over a pile of straw. As I look at the sheet, I notice a pressing in it that looks like a sleeping person. I quickly back out of the barn and continue running until I am in the middle of the meadow. I look back, and see the white dog behind me, carrying a large bone. He drops to the ground and begins to chew on the bone. I wonder what kind of bone it is.

I try to think. Who might have slept on the dirty flax sheet on the pile of straw? Was this person there last night? And where is he now? Is he in the dark forest watching me, or did he—or they—merely sleep there on their way to somewhere else?

With these thoughts in mind, I return to my bag of food and the metal container of water. I sit down and begin to eat. The white dog lies down, drops the bone, and looks at my sandwich. I break off a piece and place it in front of him. He eats it quickly, and immediately looks at my hand holding the sandwich. I share the pieces of my food until they are gone.

I drink some of the warm water and decide to walk to the cows and sheep which have moved to a wet spot near the edge of the forest. They are drinking from a small spring that bubbles out of the ground. After drinking the water, they move about and eat grass.

Because I feel very alone, I walk back to the entrance to the meadow and pass over the narrow trail surrounded by the darkness of the forest. As I emerge at the other end, I see the farm in the distance. I feel better, because I no longer feel so alone. I return to the meadow and sit down under the large birch tree where I sat earlier. Suddenly, I hear the ringing of the bell.

The animals hear it, also. The white dog runs to the animals and moves behind them. The entire herd begins to move toward me. I hurriedly count the twelve cows and thirty sheep, and I breath in relief that the white dog and I still have them all. We quickly leave the meadow and return to the farm.

My grandparents are waiting. My grandmother tells me that I did well in the forest. They herd the animals into the barn, and my grandmother begins to milk the cows. I walk to the house, and as I pass the barrel of birch sap brew, I take the tin cup off the hook, fill it, and drink. It feels good as it enters my throat. I am glad that my first day as a shepherd has gone well and that I am back at the farm. And away from the meadow surrounded by a deep forest and the dirty flax sheet spread over straw which is pressed down by a sleeping form. But since I have my white dog to protect me, I decide not to mention it to my grandparents.

After all, I am seven years old and almost an adult.

Chapter 10.

DOG IS MISSING

One morning, when I descend the ladder from my sleeping place, I notice that my large white dog is not waiting for me at the bottom. I whistle, but he doesn't come as he always has done in the past. I ask my grandmother, and she assures me that he will probably be around. After a short breakfast, I pack my sandwiches into my pockets, making sure there is something extra for my dog.

As I lead the cattle and sheep down the trail where the forest begins, I see something white hanging from a low branch of a white birch tree. I start running toward the tree, and suddenly see my dog, held up by a rope tied to his neck. He blends in with the white bark of the tree. I run to the tree, pull myself up to the branch that holds the dog, and cut the rope with my pocketknife. The lifeless body falls to the ground.

I have forgotten about my animals. I run back to the farm and tell my grandmother. She follows me down the trail to the tree and the dead body of my dog. She doesn't speak, only puts her arm around my shoulders, and holds me very tight. She tells me that some men came through the land last night. They were heading east, toward the Front. She offers no explanation. She drags the dog into a thicket, and we cover it with fir branches and tall ferns. She turns to me and tells me to be brave. She gives me a hug and starts walking toward the farm.

I head in the direction of the cattle. I think about the men and my dog. I wonder if the men are near me in the forest. I feel very alone.

Chapter 11.

JAAN, MY FRIEND

One day, when I am with the herd of cows and sheep, I hear a sound of footsteps behind me. I turn around, and I see something coming toward me, its face covered with mud and leaves that are attached to the mud. It is ugly and dreadful. As I turn to run, overcome by horrible fright, I hear the creature call out my name. When I stop—as it commands—it arrives beside me and says, "I am Jaan, your friend."

Jaan is three years older than I am, and lives on a neighboring farm. We often spend time together. He shakes my hand and tells me that he has to go and will see me again. By now, I have overcome my horrible fright. A little.

I return to my cows and sheep and wish the big white dog were with me.

Chapter 12.

WILL MY PARENTS RETURN?

It is every day that I expect my parents to return. But it does not happen. And as time goes on, I am beginning to feel that they will never return.

There are days when the neighbors visit my grandparents, and they always provide information about the approaching Germans. At the beginning of the second week of July, we are told by a visiting neighbor that the German army has advanced well into the southern part of Estonia, which is only about ninety kilometers from where we are. He says that it will probably be only a week before the German army arrives. However, it could be longer if the advancing army decides to turn east and seals off the country to the east toward the Russian border.

My grandfather tells me one day that when I take out the cows and sheep, I should stay close to the farm and not enter the forest. He tells me the retreating Russian soldiers will most likely travel under the cover of forests, rather than in an open area. I am relieved that I can follow his new directions, because I would be frightened if I were approached by Russian soldiers in the forest.

As time passes, day by day, there is no indication that the Russian or German armies are anywhere around us. And as we pass into August, I am beginning to think that the war has ended. But I wonder always about my parents.

One day in early September, my father arrives on foot. We all run to the road to greet him, and he gives me a hug, then lifts my sister, holding her tightly. And as he does this, I see tears flowing from his eyes.

I immediately think that my mother is dead. My grandmother hugs him and asks about my mother. He assures all of us that she remained in

Tallinn but will be joining us in about a week. This puts my mind at ease. He tells us the Russian army fled Tallinn on August 28, and Viljandi is also free of the Russians. He says when my mother returns, we will eventually return to Viljandi, because I will have to start school, and he hopes he will be able to return to his work at the bank.

In the evening, as the adults sit around drinking birch bark brew and discussing the events since we last saw him in Tallinn—when he stepped into the doorway and disappeared—I hear him tell of his other narrow escape that day. He says he was passing through the Old Town Square, on his way to his hiding place, when the Russians sealed all eight entrances to the Square and approached all the men to demand their papers. Unexpectedly, a great downpour of rain began, and the Russians abruptly scattered for shelter. My father fled.

I ask him what was on the page he tore out of his identity book, when we were on the bus from Piirita. He tells me that it said he should be in the Russian army.

The next morning, my father leaves on foot. As he is about to depart, several German army trucks stop at the farm. The soldiers get off and ask my father if he has seen any Russian troops. Since none of us has seen any, they drive off, after explaining that they are checking the area to make sure all the Russians have left. This is comforting.

Chapter 13.

EARLY SEPTEMBER, 1941, TO THE NEW YEAR, 1942

My mother returns early in September. It is a good surprise. We are eating lunch, and she comes in through the kitchen door. She has walked from Viljandi and is wearing old peasant clothes again. She looks thin, and at first, I don't know her. My sister runs to her, and she lifts her up and gives her a kiss. She hugs me and hugs my grandparents. Over supper she tells us what has happened to her since we saw her. She has been living in Tallinn with friends, and digging trenches for the Russian army. When the Germans came, she immediately took a train to Viljandi and walked to us. Now she says we will return to Viljandi tomorrow.

I am not happy with this news, because I will be expected to return to school. I tell my mother that I have worked as a shepherd, and I would like to continue doing this. As my grandparents hear this conversation, they both tell me that they are happy with my work, but feel that I should return to school. However, they add, they would like to have me work as a shepherd the following spring.

After a sleepless night above the barn, I join the others to leave. My grandfather will take us to Viljandi with a horse and wagon.

When we arrive in Viljandi it is afternoon, and we return to the house we left that night when there was "a knock on the door."

The door is locked with a padlock, and my mother has a key to open it. She tells me that when the Russians left, my father returned to check the house, and the lock on the door was broken. Whoever entered the building after "a knock on the door" must have broken it to get in. As we enter the house we notice many things thrown on the floor. It is a mess.

My mother tells me it is now safe to live here and that I will have to go to school again, and this news does not make me happy. She gives us ham sandwiches that she brought from Tuule Farm, and then tells my sister and me to go to bed.

My mother awakens me after a night of sleep. I wonder to myself how the cows and sheep are doing. Later in the day, we go to the school where I had attended part of first grade. We are told that the school will not start until January, because many teachers were deported, and new teachers have to be found. I am told that in January, 1942, I will be in second grade. I am happy not to go to school, but I am saddened that the reason we have no school is because many of the teachers have been sent to Siberia. Although I will not miss school, I am very careful not to show my happiness to my mother.

After a few days, my father returns and says that he will be going back to his old job as president of the bank. He adds that his Citroën auto was confiscated by the Russians and he does not expect to ever see it again. I overhear him asking my mother if there is any news of his brother Alfred, or of Marta or Hille. She says that there is none.

As time goes on, I find some of my friends whom I knew in first grade. We begin to see each other, because the days have become boring, with very little to do. One day, in front of our house, we see a Gypsy woman approaching us. As she gets close to us, she begins to wave her arms, and as she does this, she is saying something. One of my friends picks up a wooden stick and draws a cross in the sandy walk in front of her. She stops and begins to scream at us. But the words coming from her mouth make no sense. We quickly turn around and run to my house and hide behind the fence.

We see her turn around and walk back to where she came from. Later, one of my friends says that the Gypsy woman's screams were words that would bring bad luck to us, and most likely something horrible will happen to us very soon. He tells us that his grandmother told him this after he told her what happened. I wonder what will happen.

One day, my grandfather arrives with the horse and wagon. He says he has to buy some goods for the farm. I immediately ask him if I can go with him to the Tuule Farm. He asks my mother and she agrees, saying I really have very little to do until school starts in January. She packs my clothing into a bag and she, as well as my sister, gives me a hug. Before leaving, my grandfather tells me I can stay until the frost, and that I can help by again being a shepherd.

As we are about to leave, I ask my grandfather if I can hang on to the reins and drive the horse. He lets me do it, and we start out. Although I am driving the horse, he tells me to hand the reins to him if the horse gives me trouble by not following the road. But the horse behaves, because I am seven and one-half years old and almost an adult.

After about an hour, we arrive at the Tuule Farm, and as I get off the wagon, my grandmother rushes over and gives me a hug. I am happy.

I begin working as a shepherd the following day. The hours spent in the woods go by quickly, and I look forward to the evenings, when I get back to the house to sneak some birch bark brew and talk with my grandparents. I have missed the pig butchering, but they tell me all about it.

My parents do not visit, because my father no longer has the car, and it is a long walk. When the beginning of November arrives, I am ready to return to Viljandi and again spend time with friends before school begins in early January. Before I leave, however, my cousins Uno and Valdo arrive. They will be staying at the farm and will help my grandparents. They have been staying with other relatives these past months. We are very happy to see them.

Uno, who is twelve years old, will stay with my grandparents until school starts and then live with some of his other relatives. Valdo, who is sixteen, will live with us in Viljandi and attend school. He likes school, but he hopes to join an Estonian army battalion when he is seventeen in January of next year. He hopes then to be deployed to the Eastern Front. He hopes to eventually reach an unknown location in Russia, where he thinks his parents and sister are being held in a Siberian labor camp—and save them.

My grandfather returns me to Viljandi. Before long, Christmas arrives, and we celebrate the holiday because the Russians are gone. We again have a Christmas tree, which my grandfather brings from Tuule Farm. He could not do this the last two years, during the Russian occupation, and we are very glad that he can do it now. The tree is as tall as our high ceilings, and it is decorated with glass ornaments—birds, bells, and balls—and wax candles that are held in metal clips and lighted for a short time every evening.

My mother's parents, Kaarel and Liina Rand, are visiting from Pärnu. They are very friendly. My grandparents from the Tuule Farm cannot be here for Christmas because they have to care for the animals. I receive scarves and mittens from my grandparents and school supplies for the coming school year from my parents. I always receive the same thing, and I am happy with these gifts.

New Year's Eve arrives, and a girl comes to our house. She will be with my sister and me during the evening, when my parents are with friends. But I do not want them to go out. My mother tells me to go to bed and places my sister across from me in her bed, which has sides on it. My sister plays with her dolls and begins to throw them at me. I pick up one of the dolls and hold it up towards her, just out of her reach, to tease her. As she reaches over the side of her bed, she falls out and lands on the floor. She begins to scream. My mother enters our room and picks her up, but she continues to scream and tells my mother that I was holding a doll away from her, and that is why she fell.

My mother is very angry with me. My sister complains that her shoulder hurts, and begins to cry again. As my father enters the room, my mother tells him Linda should be taken to the hospital, and they both go with her, leaving the girl to stay with me. I feel guilty.

My parents and sister return in about an hour, and tell me that my sister has seriously hurt one of her shoulders, and they feel that now they cannot go out to celebrate the arrival of the New Year. They are both angry with me, and seem to blame me for keeping them from going to celebrate. But I am glad they cannot go.

The following day, some of my parents' friends come to our house, and they celebrate the arrival of the year 1942. There is much wine left in glasses, and as I spot a glass with wine left in the bottom, I drink it when no one sees me. After a few sips, I feel good again.

Chapter 14.

1942: GERMAN OCCUPATION

In the middle of January, 1942 my school year begins. I am still seven years old, and I will be in the second grade and take the following classes: Estonian Language, Religion, Mathematics, Drawing, Writing, Work Skills, and Singing.

During the first day of school, our teacher explains to us what has happened to some of our teachers. They were taken away during June of last year, and no one knows what has happened to them. I think of the "knock on the door" around the end of June, last year, when the woman told my mother, "Go they are coming," and we ran from the house and walked through the night to Tuule Farm.

The school year is moving fast, but I miss being at Tuule Farm. Occasionally, my grandfather arrives with the horse pulling him in the sleigh. Although, I would rather go to the farm, he and my parents oppose that idea. I must go to school.

Because the Russians are gone, and it is the German occupation, my father has returned to the bank. One day, I look out of the second-floor bank window. The winter is cold, and there is snow in the street. Suddenly, I see a wagon come into view being pulled by about a dozen shabby-looking Russian prisoners. The wagon has high sides, and it is filled with snow-white naked bodies of Russians.

Three German guards with rifles follow the wagon, shouting at the prisoners. One of the men pulling the wagon collapses. The wagon stops, and some prisoners near the man strip him of his meager clothes, and then toss him, with much effort, on top of the dead snow-white bodies in the wagon. The wagon continues—and then, is out of sight.

The wagon comes from a prisoner of war camp we children are aware of because it is opposite our house on Turu Street, across from the open-air square where farmers sell their crops during the summer. I feel sick at this sight, but I decide not to mention it to my father because then he might not let me visit his office again.

Before I know it, spring is near. I am now eight years old, and my sister is five years old. I cannot wait until May, when I can again return to the Tuule Farm, because my grandparents are very nice to me. They leave me alone.

The school year finally ends, and I am surprised that in all the subjects I have taken, I have received grades of five, which is perfect. My parents are very happy, and they tell me that I can return to the farm in early June.

When June arrives, my grandfather comes with the horse and wagon, and we depart for the farm immediately, because my job as a shepherd will begin the following day. When we arrive at the farm, my grandmother walks to me and gives me a hug. She says they are glad I can spend the summer with them, and this makes me happy.

I take my bag of clothing into the house, and for the time, I will have a small room to sleep in. I notice that the mattress is filled with fresh straw, because the large flax bag my grandmother was weaving for it last fall is finished. My first night at the farm is very relaxing, and I sleep well. At home, I often awaken during the night and think about school.

The next morning, my grandmother awakens me at five, and after the breakfast of oatmeal, milk, and rye bread, I take the cows and sheep into a meadow near the forest. On my first day again as a shepherd, I do get a little bored. However, I much prefer doing this job to sitting in a classroom.

One day, my cousin Valdo arrives at the Tuule Farm on his bicycle. He has been living with us in Viljandi off and on since his parents and sister were deported, and even though he likes attending school and is a good student, we are still good friends. He again tells us he plans to join the Estonian army when he becomes seventeen years old next January. The army unit will actually be part of the German army. He says he hopes, after being trained, he will be sent to the Russian Front. He continues to think that as they advance into Russia, he will eventually reach the unknown area to which his parents and sister were deported. He still hopes he can save them and have them return to Estonia.

My grandparents try to convince him he should not do this, telling him that there are many dangers involved, and he could be killed. This does not seem to cause him to change his mind. However, he tells us if his family is liberated before his seventeenth birthday, he may not have to join.

After staying on the farm a few days, Valdo returns to Viljandi where he will continue to live with my parents.

On another day, a German army truck arrives at the farm. Besides the three soldiers, there is a man dressed in old clothing. One of the soldiers tells my grandfather that this man is a Russian prisoner who has been in a camp in Viljandi. He is short, with a shaved head. Because he is not a problem, and there is no risk that he may escape, the army has decided that he can live and work on my grandparents' farm.

As they take him off the back of the truck, they explain that his name is Maxim and that he only speaks Russian. My grandparents also know Russian, and they let the soldiers know that they are glad to have him. The truck leaves, and my grandparents lead the Russian into the house. They explain to him that he will sleep in the kitchen, which has a large wood-burning brick stove reaching almost to the ceiling, that he will be given some clothing, and that he will receive three meals a day. In the summer, he will sleep on a narrow bed in the kitchen, and in the winter, he can sleep on the brick stove.

When Maxim hears of the food, he begins to nod his head, points at his mouth, and starts to smile. During the evening meal, it is obvious that he has not had much food while in the camp. The moment he fills his plate, he begins to eat very fast, and when his plate is empty, he asks my grandparents for more. I notice this, because at home I have to eat slowly, and my mother has me hold books under my elbows and tight to my sides, to slow me down and to keep my elbows off the table.

After the meal is finished, my grandfather takes Maxim into the barn and explains to him that his duties will include cleaning the manure out of the barn. When that is done for the day, he will be helping in the fields and will relieve me of my shepherd work on Sunday. Whenever a certain task is explained to him, he smiles and nods his head in approval. He is very pleasant.

When we return to the house, Maxim is given a straw-filled mattress bag, along with a blanket woven by my grandmother. She also gives him several old clothing items, and shortly we all go to bed, only to be awakened by my grandmother at five. After breakfast, we all go outside and begin our daily tasks.

I am pleased that Maxim is here. He is friendly to me and works hard. I like him. I am glad he will be taking the cows and sheep to the pasture on Sundays, because I now only have to work six days a week. On Sundays, we can take a nap. Sometimes neighbors visit, or we visit them. My grandmother serves a delicious lunch with ham, potatoes, pickles, rye bread, and her wonderful strawberry jam. She also serves cabbage, peas, beans, or tomatoes when they are ripe. The adults talk about farming and crops and the weather, and when my friend Jaan visits, the two of us just sit around and listen or talk. After supper, most evenings, I read one of my birthday books which my parents have brought to the farm.

The summer goes by quickly, and when the middle of August arrives, my grandfather takes me to Viljandi because I am about to begin the new school year. I would rather stay on the farm.

The classes I am assigned are the same as the previous school year. As school starts, I am again bored. I wish I could have stayed at the Tuule Farm with my grandparents, but there is no possibility that my parents will allow me to drop out of school.

Every day after school, I am told to return home and do my assignments for the following day. My father insists on reviewing my mathematics assignments, and if I do poorly, he becomes very upset. He tells me that I will never become a banker if I do poorly in mathematics. I want to work on the Tuule Farm, but I do not tell him this.

Before I know it, Christmas arrives, and on Christmas Eve the usual relatives come to our house, and we are all sad, because my uncle Alfred, his wife Marta, and my cousin Hille are still somewhere in Russia, and we are certain that they will not be celebrating as we are. But Valdo, almost seventeen, and his younger brother Uno, are here. This helps.

In addition to the scarves and mittens my grandmothers knitted for me and the school supplies given to me by my parents, I am given the book *Little Lord Fauntleroy*. I plan to start reading it immediately, and when I do begin this book, I find it so exciting that I have trouble putting it down when my mother interrupts to have me help bring in wood or sweep the floor.

Chapter 15.

1943: IS WAR RETURNING?

In January, 1943, the last half of the school year begins, and I am assigned the same classes as before. When snow begins to fall, I put on my high felt boots and am allowed to go skiing with my friends near the Viljandi Castle. Sometimes my mother skis, too. But when I arrive home, I always have to do school assignments. I can't wait until June, when I can again return to the farm where no one will bother me.

Time passes. When I am done with the 1943 school year, I am assigned to the third-grade level for September. In June I return to the farm, and the summer is again fun. Jaan and I visit often. I am assigned additional tasks to perform. Because I am nine years old, I can help in harvesting hay as it matures. I always sleep upstairs in the barn, and when everyone has gone to bed, I sit on top of the ladder and watch the stars above.

One evening, my grandmother says that she is planning on going into a forest to pick strawberries the following day, and she asks me if I can go along and help her. I tell her that I will be glad to do this. Maxim will take care of the cows and sheep while we are berry picking.

We leave the next afternoon carrying along baskets, blankets to sleep on, ham sandwiches, and water. We walk for at least an hour on a road, and then enter a meadow surrounded by a forest. When we arrive, we begin to pick berries and do that until dusk. My grandmother lets me eat so many of these little red berries, I cannot eat any more of them. They are delicious.

After we eat the sandwiches, my grandmother tells me that we must now go to sleep, and she prepares for me a place to sleep on top of fir branches which are on the ground. She covers me with one of the blankets, and as she lies down near me she wishes me good night, and we both fall asleep. Only to awaken as the sun begins to rise. We again eat some sandwiches and begin to pick berries. We do this until noon, at which time she empties some of the filled baskets into bags made out of a thin cloth. She ties one of the bags to my back with a piece of rope, and I am given two filled baskets to carry. She does the same for herself.

With this wonderful, but heavy, load we begin the walk back to Tuule Farm, and arrive in about two hours, after resting on the way. Once back, she empties the baskets and bags into several metal containers, and tells me that she will be making jam the next day. I love the jam she makes, because it tastes like the fresh berries, and she lets me eat as much as I want on the good bread she bakes in the huge oven in her kitchen. This is the oven Maxim sleeps on during the winter.

The summer goes quickly, and before I know it, it's fall and time for me to return to school. Again, I would rather stay on the farm.

The subjects I am taking are the same as earlier in the year, and I finally realize that there is no way of avoiding school, and I simply have to get along. I have friends. But I cannot like school.

During the late fall of 1943, I hear adults talking again about the war, which has been gone for awhile, as far as my life is concerned. Now it seems that the German attack on Russia is beginning to take a turn, and the adults are again whispering about the danger of war returning to us. I try to listen as they talk, but they keep their voices down when children are near.

One day in December, my cousin Valdo, who has continued to live with us while attending the gymnasium, tells us that he has decided to join the Estonian army attached to the German army. After our Christmas, my grandparents from the farm and several other relatives, including Valdo's brother Uno, gather at our house in Viljandi to wish Valdo good-bye. It is a sad gathering. We all know that he will be sent to the Russian Front before long, and I wonder if I will ever see him again. We have not seen or heard from his mother and father and sister.

As Valdo leaves for the army, I am aware of war, once more. Although I have not been very aware of it since the autumn of 1941, I now realize there are very few times in my life when I have not been reminded of war.

The school year begins in January, 1944. Not a day passes in which I am unaware that the Russian army will probably return. Increasingly, I hear my parents talking in whispers about what we should do if the war returns to where we are. I try to eavesdrop, but as they quit talking when children are near, I cannot be sure of what they are saying.

However, the school year passes quickly, and my grades are good, in spite of the fact that I do not like school. Before long, thank goodness, it is again time to go to the Tuule Farm and become a shepherd.

Besides being a shepherd, I am allowed to drive the team of horses as we begin to cut the hay fields, because I am now ten years old. I like this work because it makes me feel older and of more help to my grandparents.

Whenever my parents visit, they talk in whispers to my grandparents, and now I often can hear that they are worried about the Front approaching from the East. I remember we enjoyed over two years without being very aware of war. Now, we have again reached a time when war is returning quickly in this summer of 1944. Their whispers tell me this.

One morning, my grandfather asks me to help with rolling up the dried hay. He tells me that Maxim, who is still working and living on the farm, can take the animals to their pasture.

I immediately agree to help with the hay, and my grandfather walks one of the horses to the hay field that has been cut and hitches it to the rake. He tells me to climb on the rake and sit on the metal seat behind the horse, and above the rake. He hands me the reins and tells me what to do to work the rake.

After his instruction, I move the reins, and the horse begins to walk. I guide him to the edge of the field and gently slap the reins against his back. As he begins to move down the cut hayfield, the curved metal rake behind me rolls up the hay underneath it. As soon as a roll of hay fills it, the rake rises, and a roll of hay is left behind.

My grandfather nods his head in my direction and walks back to the barn. I continue doing my new job. It seems like easy work.

However, without warning, the horse stumbles. After he rights himself, he takes off running toward the barn. I pull on the reins, but accidentally, they drop out of my hands. The horse keeps running, and the rake keeps lifting and lowering. As we hit a bump in the field, I fall to the ground beneath the rake, and my right hand is run over by one of the heavy iron wheels. Fortunately, the rake rises as it passes over me, but I am left lying on the ground with great pain in my right hand. I look at my hand and see much blood coming from my first finger, which is now bent at a strange angle.

When I get to the farm, running, I see that my grandfather has stopped the horse. My grandmother comes running toward me. She holds my right hand and takes me into the kitchen, where she washes my finger with her homemade soap, and water. She gets a piece of cloth and walks me to the yard near the barn. Then she tells me to wait while she enters the pigpen. She bends down, places a piece of pig manure on the cloth, returns to me, and wraps the cloth around my finger. She tells me to hold this injured hand near my waist, and adds that she will be changing the cloth three times a day.

She also tells me that I have broken my finger and it is badly cut, but it should feel better after a few days. She says I will have pain for a few days, but she will give me some birch bark beer to drink, and this will help me sleep at night. I wish I could have some right now.

In a few days, as my grandmother continues to wrap my hand with the pig-manure bandage, my swollen, twisted finger begins to feel better. However, I notice that it smells like pig manure. The birch bark beer she gives me makes me forget about the pain, and after about a week, my finger no longer hurts. I think birch bark beer is very good for healing wounds.

One weekend, when my parents visit, I decide not to tell them about my injured finger because it might make them angry with me. When I am with them, I put my right hand in the side pocket of my pants. They never notice.

Chapter 16.

THUNDER TO THE EAST: MIDSUMMER, 1944

I am again sitting at the top of the ladder. It is late, and I cannot sleep. I'm looking to the east. I see flashes of lightning. Occasionally, I hear the thunder, but the sky is clear. And I know it's not a storm that's approaching. I know it's the Front. I suddenly realize that it is coming closer. I go to the house, hoping my grandparents are still awake. I must talk to them about this thunder, which we have not heard before.

As I enter my grandparents' room, my grandmother awakens and asks me why I am not sleeping. I tell her about the thunder to the east. She follows me to the barn and we listen. We see flashes of light followed by a faint noise. She tells me that it's the Front and explains that the noise is louder because it is very quiet outside, and I should not worry.

I walk her to the house, and she places her arm around my shoulders and gives me a hug. She enters the house, and I begin to walk to the barn. But I stop next to the barrel of birch bark beer around the corner. I fill the tin cup that is always hanging on the wooden spigot. I drink it all, replace the cup, and return to the barn. As I climb the ladder, I look to the east. There is no lightning. I climb up and lie down on the flax bag. I feel better.

Chapter 17.

THE EASTERN FRONT ADVANCES, EARLY AUGUST, 1944

It is early August, 1944. In the evening, when dusk arrives around ten, I watch the eastern sky. It is filled with lightning. But I know it is more than that. It is the Eastern Front approaching. It is now well-known that the Russians are coming back. The adults whisper when they look to the east, and I hear that the Russians are only twenty kilometers from us. And what looks like lightning are actually artillery flashes beyond Lake Võrtsu to our east about twenty kilometers.

The Front is holding, so I am not worried. But adults are continually talking about the war that has somehow changed and is returning. They have forgotten to whisper. I think there probably won't be school in four weeks. This thought alone offsets any occasional fears that I might have.

I keep leaving my sleeping place when darkness comes. I sit on the upper end of the ladder and look to the east and the soundless flashes of light. When I get very tired, I crawl into my large bag and fall asleep—only to be awakened at five in the morning, when I take the twelve cows and thirty sheep to the pasture surrounded by the dark forest of birch and fir trees. There I stay, until four in the afternoon, when I again drive the livestock back to the barn so that my grandmother can milk the cows. I have done this for four summers, since I was seven years old, and they said I was almost an adult. I want to be a help to my grandparents. I feel they like me. And I like them.

Chapter 18.

DAY OF DEPARTURE, MIDDLE OF AUGUST, 1944

The artillery flashes at night seem to be closer from the east. I hear rumbling even during the day. I just know that the Eastern Front is coming closer and closer. It is no longer holding.

My parents and my sister are visiting and have been here for a few days now. One day, my mother's parents, who live in Pärnu, arrive at the farm in a horse-drawn wagon. After they get off, the driver of the wagon leaves. I don't know this man who brought them. The adults gather, and my grandfather serves his homemade brew. Someone brings out a bottle of vodka, and the adults pass it around and drink from it. They speak in whispers. When I move closer to the group, to hear the conversation, they stop.

I walk to the barrel of homemade brew and fill the cup that hangs from the hook. I take the cup and walk behind the house, out of sight of the adults. I drink the bitter fluid, and I feel good. This liquid is like magic. I have begun to associate it with happiness. I no longer worry about the "thunder to the east."

Suddenly, I hear my mother call my name. I run to the group of adults, still holding the now empty cup. My mother asks me what I am doing with the cup. I tell her that I used it in the house, to drink some water. She seems satisfied with my story.

My father approaches and tells me that the Russian army is very close, and we must leave as soon as it gets dark. It is quickly getting dark. I look at my grandmother, the one who helped me cover my dead dog with fir boughs. She is crying. As she looks at me, she places her hands under her apron, raises the apron to her face, and wipes the tears from her eyes.

I run to her, and she drops to her knees and embraces me with both arms. I feel tears running down my face. I embrace her and suddenly realize that this is a good-bye that is forever—and not just a separation from which one hopes to return. Everyone is hugging each other—and crying.

Suddenly, my grandfather appears with a horse and wagon. My father places suitcases on the wagon and helps my mother and sister onto the wagon. He then climbs on board and motions to me to climb on. I look at my grandmother, and she is still crying. I suddenly realize that I want to stay. I am leaving behind something that I will miss forever, and I realize I will never see them or Tuule Farm again. I stand and refuse to leave. I ignore my father's order to climb on board. My grandmother walks to me and tells me that I must go. And after hearing her words, I climb on.

Chapter 19.

JOURNEY THROUGH THE NIGHT

Once on the wagon, I sit down, facing my relatives who are left behind. They are now waving and in tears. My grandfather jerks the horse's reins, and the wagon pulls away. We are quickly out of sight of the people left behind. It is dark now, and I see flashes of light to the east, followed by distant thunder.

We enter the narrow road through the thick forest. As we pass through a cluster of houses, a man approaches the wagon, and my grandfather pulls on the reins. The wagon comes to a halt, and the man steps next to my grandfather. They whisper, the man waves, and the wagon begins to move.

After what seems an eternity, we enter Viljandi. It is nearly midnight, and the houses are dark. I wonder why these people are asleep, and we are traveling through the warm August night. I see a man and woman walking along a street holding hands. We pass them, and the man waves. We are fleeing, but they do not seem worried.

As we approach the center of Viljandi, we pass my father's bank. My thoughts drift back to the sight of a wagon filled with cold, snow-white bodies. Suddenly, I see people gathered around an open truck down the street. My grandfather stops the wagon near them, and my father tells us to take our bags and climb down.

My sister has fallen asleep in my mother's arms, and as she is awakened, she begins to cry. We get off the wagon, and my grandfather approaches me. He holds out his hand, and I press mine into his. He looks at me and smiles—and thanks me for helping and being a good shepherd. I thank him for taking care of me. And I suddenly know, that after this good-bye, I will never see him again. He drops my hand, walks to my sister, picks her up, and kisses her. He then hugs my father and my mother and climbs on the wagon. As he sits down, the horse begins to move in a circle, heading away from us. Then he is gone.

My father asks me to follow him. We walk a short distance away from the waiting truck. He bends down and gives me a hug. He tells me that because the Russians will be back very soon, my mother, sister, and I must try to escape to Finland, Sweden, or Germany. He says that the truck will take us to Tallinn. Because he cannot leave, he tells me that I am now an adult, and I should do whatever is needed to help my mother and sister. I nod. And we return to the waiting truck.

My father says to climb on the truck, which seems to be loaded with women and children. He hands me the bags that we brought along from the farm. He then lifts my sister onto the truck, and he helps my mother climb on board. He again tells me he is staying, but will follow us in a few days.

The driver approaches and announces that we will be leaving shortly. There are people standing around the truck. I see a woman wipe her eyes with the back of her hand. I suddenly see a coffin, made of white boards. It is partially hidden by bags of belongings placed over it. My mother is seated on the floor of the truck with my sister cradled in her arms. I look around, but there is very little room for me to sit. A woman has noticed my problem. She suddenly points at me and speaks to the people huddled on the floor. She says, "Let's put the boy in the coffin." Some of the people laugh. The woman lifts the cover of the coffin with great difficulty because of the bags on top, and says, "There's no one in it, and it would be warm." My mother quickly speaks up and says, "Leave the boy alone." I am relieved. The thought of riding in a coffin through the night scares me. The woman then closes the coffin cover, gives me a hug, and tells me that I can sit on the end of the coffin. I follow her suggestion.

Quickly, the driver starts the truck by using a crank device in front of the engine. The truck roars, the driver gets in, and we take off. My father, along with the other people left behind, is waving. As the truck enters a curve, they fade into darkness, and are gone.

The truck is without headlights to avoid attracting Russian aircraft. We pass through dark streets and enter a road leading into a forest. Some of the people begin to speak in whispers, and I try to close my eyes. But I am wide awake. I look around. Some people seem to be sleeping with their heads leaning against a companion's shoulder. A baby starts to cry. But this sound is silenced by the roar of the truck and the rumbling noise made by its tires.

Suddenly, the truck slows. And stops. I stand up and look ahead. The road is blocked by German army vehicles. I see shadowy forms standing in small groups. Several soldiers approach the truck with weapons pointed at the truck. One of the soldiers speaks to the driver, who then steps out of the cab. They speak in low tones. The driver takes out a cigarette from his breast pocket, places it in his mouth, lights it, and then hands it to the soldier, who immediately puts it in his mouth. The lighted cigarette illuminates the darkness. The soldier again speaks to the driver, who then walks to the truck, opens the door, and removes a bottle. He hands it to the soldier, who lifts his right hand to his head as though giving a salute. The driver then gets into the cab and starts again down the road, weaving his way around an endless convoy of German army trucks.

Once past the trucks, he shifts gears, and as I look back, the last of the trucks dims from sight, interrupted by lighted cigarettes in the mouths of soldiers still looking toward us. But after a short moment, the glow of the cigarettes is gone, and we are again in darkness.

I fall asleep lying down on top of the coffin, with my head resting on bags of clothing belonging to other passengers. When I awaken, I am cold, and it is raining. No one seems to be concerned, and I think that wherever this journey leads, there will be situations far worse than a rain in August.

As the truck enters Tallinn, early morning has arrived. We travel past buildings that are in ruins. I ask my mother why things have changed since our visit here in June of 1941, and she tells me that earlier this spring a large part was destroyed by Russian bombers.

I am again worried because we have left the Tuule Farm where I felt comfortable. Now I am part of another world. My mother senses my concern and tells me that we will be living outside of Tallinn, in the country, and it will be safer there.

Abruptly, the truck stops in the center of Tallinn. It is an open area surrounded by old buildings. We climb off the truck. My mother tells me that, from now on, I will be carrying three bags, one strapped to my back and one in each hand. I nod in her direction, and do as told. She adds that she will only be able to carry one bag because she has to hold onto my sister.

We leave the cobblestoned square surrounded by old buildings, and I suddenly realize that I was here in June of 1941, when the war began three years ago. It was here that my father left us, after our day in Piirita, where we heard on the radio that the Germans had attacked the Russians.

We reach a railroad station, and my mother tells me we will be living in a house in Piirita, about ten kilometers from Tallinn. After an hour's wait, we board a train and arrive at our destination in about an hour, after many stops. There, we walk a short distance, and I recognize the house where we huddled in a deep hole with planes overhead, way back in June of 1941. I realize that after about three years of feeling good, things have again changed. And I am scared, and confused.

My mother's voice brings me out of my thoughts. As she unlocks the door with a key from her coat pocket, she instructs me to drop my bags and follow her. I enter the house, look around, return to my bags, and bring them inside. She tells me to leave them in a corner of the room and stay with my sister, because she has to walk to a store in Piirita to buy some bread and potatoes. I nod my head in her direction, and she leaves. My sister stumbles to a corner of the room, lies down, and before long is asleep. I go outside and sit on the wooden steps and try to make sense out of the day. Much has happened, and now I am worried and afraid, as well as confused.

Chapter 20.

FIRST DAY IN PIIRITA

I think of the Tuule Farm, which we left last night. After traveling all night, we have reached our destination late this day. I heard my mother say it was 120 kilometers to Tallinn from Viljandi. That is a long journey from home. I wonder what my grandparents are doing. Who is taking care of the cows and sheep? I wish I could go back.

I see my mother approaching from a distance, carrying a bag. I quickly leave the steps I've been sitting on and go inside, where my sister is sleeping on the floor. As my mother enters, she places the bag on a table, goes into another room, and returns with a blanket which she places on my sleeping sister. Next, she opens the bag she carried during our trip and takes out a large item wrapped in white cloth. She removes a ham from the wrapping and places it on the table with the things she has just bought—some potatoes and carrots and a bottle with a cork showing. She takes a glass off a shelf, removes the cork, pours the red liquid into the glass, and drinks from it.

She then leaves the room, but the red liquid in the open bottle remains on the table. I look at it closely and wonder what it is. I think it is wine. Hearing my mother in the kitchen, I quickly walk to the table, grasp the bottle with both hands, raise it to my open mouth, and drink from it as though it were water. The sweet liquid fills my mouth, and I swallow it slowly. I place the bottle on the table and walk out of the house. I feel better as I sit on the steps.

My thoughts again return to my grandparents at the farm we left only yesterday. But it seems much longer. I wish that I could somehow return. I think of the German army trucks we met on the way. Could I possibly leave this place, catch a train to Tallinn, and then walk, hoping that I could somehow find a way? Maybe with another group of trucks, I could ask to get a ride.

I hear the door open behind me, and my mother tells me to come into the house. I follow her. I look at the bottle on the table, and wish I could have some more of the sweet liquid that somehow made me feel good. The feeling it gave me is much the same as I got from drinking my grandfather's homemade brew. My mother tells me and my sister that we can eat. In the kitchen, we look at the food. We haven't eaten for a day, but I'm not hungry. A lonely feeling seems to have overtaken me. I eat a piece of ham, along with a potato and bread. But my thoughts are not with the meal.

The rest of the day, nothing happens. When darkness falls, my mother tells me not to turn on any lights, because it might attract Russian planes. I leave the house, walk up a street, and everything is in darkness. I return to the dark house and hear my mother and sister in another room. As I enter, my mother tells me to get ready for bed. I'm told to sleep in an adjoining room. My mother and sister will share another bed upstairs. I remove my shoes and climb under a blanket. I hear my mother and sister talking upstairs, and then there is silence.

I am unable to fall asleep, and suddenly think of the bottle of wine. I get out of bed and approach the table, feel the bottle with both hands—and grasp it. I drink from it, place it down, and return to my bed. In a short while, I am asleep.

Chapter 21.

DAYS IN PIIRITA AS AUGUST CONTINUES

The days become boring. Some days we take a train to Tallinn and walk the streets. We walk to the Tallinn Harbor, and it is filled with German ships. The days have gotten warm. It is mid-August, and I am bored because I have nothing to do. I miss the Tuule Farm. I miss my grandparents. But I know I cannot return.

One day, at the harbor, my mother approaches a German naval officer standing next to a gangplank leading on board one of the ships. They converse in German. My mother looks over and tells me to take my sister up the dock for a walk. I do exactly as told. My sister and I stand next to a ship and watch it being loaded. I think my mother is asking the naval officer about plans to leave Estonia for Germany.

Quickly, my mother approaches and says that we are going back to Piirita. The train we take is very crowded, with people hanging onto the sides of cars. I wonder where they are going. Finally, we arrive in Piirita and return to the house. My mother tells me that my father will be visiting in a few days. This is good news.

The days are boring. There is nothing to do. I wander the streets of Piirita. I almost welcome the sounds of planes overhead, even if they might be unfriendly. I wish I had some books to read, but we have none. They would be too heavy to carry.

My mother, sister, and I visit Piirita to buy food. One day, while we are there, I see a column of soldiers approaching from a distance. As they come nearer at a fast march, they create a column of dust, and we step aside to let them pass. Suddenly, I see a familiar face among the soldiers. It's my cousin Valdo whom we haven't seen since last December—not since he joined the Estonian army to fight on the Eastern Front, hoping to rescue his parents and sister who were deported to Siberia in June, 1941.

We call to him and start to walk at a fast pace next to him, trying to find out where he is going. But as he continues marching, he shouts that his destination is not known. He quickly bends down, picks up my sister, and gives her a hug. After putting her down, he holds onto my mother's arm and to mine, and as we lose the grip of his hand, he briefly looks back.

We stand and watch the column of soldiers keep moving away and eventually disappear into a column of dust. I look at my mother and sister. Both have tears in their eyes, and I wonder if we will ever see Valdo again.

Chapter 22.

MY FATHER ARRIVES IN PIIRITA, AND THE NEXT DAY WE LEAVE ESTONIA

My father arrives one morning, and we are happy to see him. He speaks to my mother in whispers. I try to hear what they are saying but have no luck. Whenever I approach them, they move to another room.

That night, my mother begins to pack clothing. She sets some of my clothing on a chair, two of every piece of clothing. She does the same with my sister's clothes.

When darkness falls, my sister and I are told to go to bed. I protest, but it's no use. I finally lie down, but I cannot sleep. I hear planes overhead, but there are no sirens. I almost wish the sirens would go off, because then we would be allowed to get up and go into the basement. I finally fall asleep.

When morning comes, I am awakened by my mother. My father enters the room and tells me that my mother, my sister, and I will be returning to the harbor later today, and we will be going to Germany. He tells me that he cannot go with us now but will join us later. When I ask why he can't go with us, he explains that men older than sixteen years are not allowed to leave, because they will have to join the German army and defend our country against the approaching Russians.

My mother tells me to get dressed and put on all the clothing that she placed on the chair yesterday. She says that I will be carrying a backpack and two suitcases. We can only take whatever we can carry, and since she will have to carry my sister at times, she will not be able to take a large suitcase.

I get dressed as told, and find myself wearing two pairs of pants, two shirts, two pairs of underwear, and two pairs of socks. I am also expected to wear a winter coat and a hat, the only single items of clothing I will be wearing. It is still August. And warm.

My father tells me to follow him into the kitchen, and he fastens the backpack over my shoulders. Something hard inside it hurts my back. He then tells me to pick up the two suitcases. They are heavy, but I say nothing. He says that we will be leaving shortly, but not before we eat breakfast.

We all sit down around the table to eat. There is ham and bread, but I cannot eat. This unknown journey frightens me. I force myself to eat a slice of ham. It rolls around in my mouth. I wish I could spit it out. Finally, I swallow. My father tells me that I should eat, because it could be a long time before we have a chance to eat a full meal.

After clearing the table, my mother washes the dishes. There is a large piece of ham left. She unties my backpack and forces it into the bag. She ties the strings carefully and tells me to put on my overcoat. I do as told, and she places the pack over my arms and shoulders. She then tells me to pick up the suitcases and wait outside. As I leave the house, she begins to dress my sister. I notice that my mother is wearing two dresses, and as I look back, she is putting on a winter coat.

I go outside into the warm August sunlight and sit on the steps. I'm hot. But I realize that there is really nothing I can do. My thoughts keep drifting back to Tuule Farm, and I wonder what my grandparents are doing. I worry about them, and I am filled with sadness.

When I hear the door open behind me, I get up. My father is carrying a small red suitcase, and my mother is holding my sister by her arm. My father turns and locks the door to the house, then puts the key in his pocket. As I pick up the suitcases, my father tells me that we will take the train to Tallinn. We leave the yard and turn onto the road that will take us to the station.

The train is not crowded, and after a short ride, we arrive in Tallinn. I never bothered to take off my backpack, and I only have to pick up the two suitcases assigned to me. My father picks up my sister, and my mother is carrying the small red suitcase. We follow my father, who heads toward the harbor.

The walk takes half an hour, and when we arrive, I am exhausted. My arms and my back hurt. But I know I cannot complain, because this is a task assigned to me, and I only hope, wherever our destination, getting there will not involve much walking.

We see a huge ship before us. My father says that it's called the Moltkefels. He approaches a German naval officer at the bottom of a gangplank and shows him some papers. The officer examines the papers and tells my father that he can board with us, but when the ship's whistle blows, he must immediately leave the ship.

We walk up the steep gangplank. I have to hang onto the handrail to support myself, because the weight of the backpack pulls me backwards. I struggle. But we all make it to the deck of the ship. I see mostly women with children. They are huddled in small groups. There are some men, and they seem to be talking to members of other huddled groups. There are hundreds of people crowding the deck.

We move on. My father tells me to take off my pack and sit down on a suitcase. I do as I am told, but I would rather wander around on the deck. I see a crane loading huge wood boxes onto the deck. As they drop, men in military uniforms unfasten the cable and push the boxes to an out-of-the-way area. I wonder what is inside these boxes. I hope they contain food, later to be given to the passengers.

Time passes. As I look back at the city with its church towers, I see the warm sun slowly sinking beyond these buildings. We have been on the deck of this ship, the Moltkefels, for several hours, and the loading on deck has stopped. Now I hear the ship's whistle blow. It is a deep, loud sound that stops and starts several times. My eyes move to my parents, with my sister between them, seated on a metal box attached to the deck of the ship.

Quickly, my father stands and walks up to me. I stand, and he sinks to his knees and embraces me. He hangs on and whispers, "Good-bye." But he adds that he will see me again very soon. As my father releases his hold, he gets up and walks to my sister. He picks her up and holds her tight. Suddenly, I see tears in his eyes. Then he walks to my mother, and she embraces both my father and sister. My mother is crying. As I look around, people in small groups are hugging each other with tears flowing down their faces. I know that this is good-bye for everyone. I instantly wonder if I will ever see my father again.

I wish we could all leave the ship and return to the Tuule Farm and be with my grandparents.

I suddenly begin to cry. I know that this is wrong. After all, I am older now—over ten years old—going on a journey to somewhere carrying two heavy bags and wearing a heavy backpack. I remember my father saying I must help my mother and sister and be an adult. I quickly wipe away my tears and try to see this journey as a new adventure.

Abruptly, the ship's whistle blows again, and my father turns and walks away, heading to the gangplank. I look around, and all the men who have been standing on the deck also begin to leave. They descend the steep gangplank to the dock below.

I run to the harbor side of the ship. My mother yells not to go. I go, regardless of her order. I look down. The men are walking away. Some look back. I see my father walking away. He does not look back. I hope he will. He does not. I turn around. My mother is sitting on a metal box, with my sister on her lap. I see tears flowing down my mother's cheeks. I walk to her and put my hand on her shoulder, and she looks up and our eyes meet. In that instant, I grow up.

Chapter 23.

CROSSING THE BALTIC SEA TO GERMANY

Within a moment, the deck of the ship comes to life. Sailors in uniform enter the area where women and children are huddled. We are instructed, in German, to move into the deck-level cargo hold of the freighter. This huge room is filled with wooden platforms with low sides around them. The platforms are large enough to make a sleeping area for at least four people, and the low sides are to keep them from rolling off. We are told to pick one of these bare spaces and place our luggage on the makeshift beds. I gladly drop my backpack and two suitcases. My mother opens one of the suitcases and removes a lightweight wool blanket that I recognize as one my grandmother has woven. It has a design of lighter and darker shades of grey. My mother instructs my sister to climb onto the makeshift bed. It is only about thirty centimeters off the floor. She tells her to lie down and she covers her with the blanket.

As soon as this is done, my sister falls asleep. My mother sits down next to my sister and tells me that I can go on deck, but she orders me not to go too far from our opening to the deck, which is only about a meter from our makeshift bed. I immediately go onto the deck.

I walk to the port side of the ship, lean over the side, and see a German staff car pull up to the gangplank. The driver opens the rear door and two naval officers emerge. The driver then removes some bags from the trunk, hands them to a waiting sailor, salutes, promptly reenters the car, and drives off. The two officers ascend the gangplank with the sailor carrying their bags. As soon as they are on board, the ship's whistle blows, sailors on deck set about removing the gangplanks, and several men unfasten chains that anchor the ship to the dock.

I hear a rumble coming from within the ship, and the deck begins to vibrate. I run to the other side and see two tugboats attached with heavy ropes to the ship. They begin to move, pulling the ship with them into the harbor, and before I know it, we are drifting away from the land that, a few hours before, I had walked on.

I look around, and see women and children huddled on the side facing the harbor. They are looking out toward the city that we are leaving. As I look at them, I see tears flowing down their cheeks. I can tell that they all are leaving something behind, and were it not for the war coming closer with every day and night, all of us would rather stay. I realize that from now on, any chance of returning to the Tuule Farm is out of the question—I probably will never see my grandparents again.

As I emerge from my thoughts, the ship begins to vibrate more. I again hear the ship's whistle, run to the rear of the ship, and see one of the tugboats being detached. I look out at the Gulf of Finland and see the other tugboat heading toward the harbor that we just left. The Moltkefels is now under her own power.

She is heading out into open waters. I look back and see the church steeples of Tallinn falling behind, with the sinking sun reflecting off them. This, to me, is now a final good-bye. I keep looking back at the shoreline as it begins to fade into the distance. I realize that we are leaving a war, but at the same time, we are going to Germany where another war is being fought. I think of my mother's distant relative who lives somewhere west of Berlin. I wonder if we will go there. At least knowing of this relative gives me some comfort. But not enough to do away with the empty feeling.

The ship is beginning to feel the affect of larger waves, and I seem to be losing control of my balance. I return to the cargo area where we will be sleeping. My sister is still asleep, but my mother is awake, sitting and staring into the emptiness of the ship's hold. I hear children crying, but I know that I am no longer one of them. I have been assigned the duties of carrying a backpack and two suitcases—our father is gone—and I know that I am now an adult, expected to do certain things that are usually assigned to adults.

A sailor enters from the deck and announces that soup and bread will be served. We are instructed to go on deck and wait for the food to arrive. My mother awakens my sister, who at first refuses to get up. But then she does, and we walk out to the deck and wait with the others.

A group of sailors arrives carrying large steaming caldrons. Others are carrying boxes filled with slices of bread. When these items are in place, we are told to line up near the steaming caldrons. At the start of the line there are metal bowls, each with a long handle attached, and spoons. The sailors arrive with large ladles in hand and motion to the waiting women and children to move forward. We are among the first in line. I walk up to the first steaming caldron and hold out the metal container. A sailor fills it with a thin soup. He hands me a slice of dark bread and motions for me to move on. At the end of the row of caldrons, another sailor tells me that when I'm finished with the soup, I can return, rinse the soup container in a steaming kettle nearby, and then get some water to drink. He tells each person that we are to keep the containers and spoons for the next day.

I do as I am told and move back inside, placing the soup container and bread on the makeshift bed. I return to the food line, and as my sister is served, I carry her soup inside. My mother follows. We all sit down on the edge of the bunk. I eat my bread first and then taste the soup. It's thin but warm, with vegetable pieces floating in it. It gives me some warmth as it goes down. I actually like it, although it contains no meat and very few vegetables.

I look over to my sister. She refuses to eat the soup. My mother insists that she eat and helps her by filling a spoon and bringing it to her mouth. My sister finally takes the spoon and begins to feed herself. After a while, she stops eating and hands the container with the remaining soup to me. I take it from her and finish it. After we have eaten, my mother instructs me to take the three containers and spoons back on deck and wash them in the kettle, which is no longer steaming. I do as I'm told, filling my own container with water. When I return, I place the container of water and the empty, but now clean containers on the bunk.

Before long, the ship's hold, filled with women and children, is in complete darkness. However, there is the sound of vibrating engines, crying children, and hushed women's voices. I walk out the opening to the ship's deck. Darkness is everywhere. I look up, and there are no lights coming from the cabins above. I see a group of shadows near the bow of the ship. They are talking and smoking cigarettes, which seem to illuminate the darkness around them.

I approach the group, and sit on an elevated platform about ten paces from them, hoping that they will approach me and talk to me about this journey which is so new to me. I have many questions, but no answers. I have heard somewhere about Russian planes attacking transport ships, similar to the one we're on, and I would like to know what has happened to the people on board when such an attack occurred. But I am reluctant to approach the sailors and ask, although fortunately, I do know the German language from studying it in school for nearly three years. I can hear that, from now on, everyone will be speaking German.

Unexpectedly, one of the sailors approaches me and asks me if I understand German. I say that I do. He asks me if I am alone, and I tell him that I am traveling with my mother and young sister. He tells me that I am lucky not to be without my family. I feel he is right.

As he is about to return to his group, I ask him about the Russian planes attacking these ships. He tells me that it has happened, but I should not worry because there is usually a warning, which allows the anti-aircraft crews to man their stations and, with luck, fire at the approaching planes and shoot them down.

I tell him that I must return to the ship's hold where my mother and sister are, explaining that my mother, most likely, is wondering where I am. He nods, and as I turn to walk away, he touches my shoulder and tells me to be brave. He then walks to the group of sailors toward the front of the ship, and I return to the hold and our makeshift bed. And I remember his advice to be brave.

The hold remains in almost total darkness. The only signs of life are a child crying and women whispering. I walk to our makeshift bed, where my mother and sister are asleep. I walk to an open space which becomes visible as my eyes adjust to the lack of light. I find my backpack and move it to the end of the open space, near the back of the bed. I lie down with my head resting on the backpack and close my eyes. I hope to fall asleep and escape thoughts of what lies ahead. My thoughts drift back to the Tuule Farm and to my grandparents. I think of the thunder to the east. And I wonder if the Front has now reached them and I think of what might be happening to them. I have heard stories of the Russian troops burning everything in their path. I wonder if they are still alive, or if they have been killed in a war that has been going on for most of my life.

I try to think what peace is like. I try to picture a place with no sirens and no planes overhead—no columns of weary troops marching down a dusty road. And I cannot picture such a place. I only see war. I do not feel like a child. I know I have somehow become an adult. I am expected to carry two heavy bags and a backpack somewhere, to a destination that I do not know.

Finally, I fall asleep.

Chapter 24.

VOYAGE ON THE MOLTKEFELS CONTINUES

I'm awakened by the loud voice of a German sailor standing in the doorway to the deck. He instructs us to go on deck and be served food. The ship's hold seems to be unsteady. It's rocking slowly back and forth. I get out of the makeshift bed and immediately feel dizzy. I try to walk, but the rocking motion of the ship causes me to stagger.

My mother and sister have awakened, and they are sitting up. I tell them we will be served food, but I warn them that the ship is rocking, and they should be careful not to fall. Now I feel I am somehow taking care of them. This makes me feel better.

We move to the deck and stand in line with the others, holding the tin containers and spoons. The sailors are handing out two slices of dark bread to each person. There is a large steaming kettle, and as I pass it a sailor pours a dark liquid into my tin container. It is coffee. I have never had coffee before, but I accept it.

We walk back to the ship's hold and sit on the bunk. We are lucky because our bunk is near the door, and we have more light. My mother opens the top of my backpack and removes the ham wrapped in a linen cloth. She tears off a piece and hands it to me. She also gives my sister a piece and takes a piece for herself, and we all eat the bread and the ham. After I've finished, I take a drink of coffee. It is bitter but warm. I realize that by drinking coffee at my age, I am more of an adult.

After going to a common toilet at the other end of the hold, I return to our makeshift bed. My mother is telling my sister something, but I can't hear the conversation. I tell her that I am going on deck, and she warns me to be careful. I nod and leave through the doorway to the deck.

I walk past the feeding line, trying to keep my balance on the rocking ship. As the front of the ship rises, I lose my balance and have to take a step backwards. To keep this from happening again, I make my way to the side of the ship, then hang onto the railing with my left arm as I move toward the front. When the front of the ship drops, I lose my balance and run ahead. I finally make it to the bow of the ship, and by hooking my arms over the railing, I have a steady view to the front.

As I look down, I see two small ships cruising in front of our cargo ship. They are attached to each other by heavy metal cables and they are dragging a metal screen between them through the water. There is a German sailor to the right of me, scanning the surface of the stormy Baltic Sea with binoculars. I approach him and ask about the small ships to our front. He turns, drops his binoculars down, and tells me that they are minesweepers. Then he raises his binoculars again and begins to scan the distance. I'm curious about his role of watching the rough seas with binoculars, but I decide not to bother him again, and instead, begin my walk back to the hold. This time I stay in the middle, but walk with great difficulty. I occasionally step back to reach a balance as the ship rocks, with the front rising and then crashing down.

In the hold, my mother and sister are asleep on the makeshift bed. I sit on the edge of the bed and my thoughts leave the ship. I'm back at Tuule Farm. It's a sunny day, and I'm at the edge of the forest in a meadow, sitting against a tree, watching the cows and sheep. And I'm suddenly happy again. Fear of the unknown has left me, and with these thoughts in my mind, I lie down at the edge of my sleeping space, place my head on the backpack, and drift off to sleep.

I'm awakened by a loud siren. I jump up and run onto the deck. I hear a plane. And the anti-aircraft guns begin to rattle. As I look up to the sky, I see a plane fly over the ship. And as it passes, I see a huge splash in the sea out in front of the ship. The plane disappears into the distant sky. There are sailors on deck wearing life jackets, and I ask one of them what happened. He pauses to tell me a Russian plane attacked the Moltkefels. But missed. The huge splash in the sea was a bomb intended for the ship. The sailor walks off, untying his life jacket. I now realize that the crew puts on the jackets whenever there is a danger to the ship. I enter the hold of the ship— thinking where are the life jackets for the passengers?

My thoughts are interrupted by my mother who asks me what happened, and I tell her. She warns me that, if a situation like I described happens again, I should not go on the open deck again. I do not answer her. Instead, I lie down, close my eyes, and in no time, fall asleep.

I'm awakened by music coming from the deck. My mother and sister are asleep. I get up and walk outside. I see a man playing an accordion. He has one whole leg, and the other is severed below the knee. His pants leg is folded back over the knee and tied above the knee with a piece of rope. He is leaning against a metal platform near the side of the ship, and his crutches are nearby on the deck. As the ship rocks, he is able to keep his balance. The music goes on, and some women and children are gathering around him. The small group surrounding the man faces him. But no one is singing, or even swinging, to the tunes.

Without any warning, the ship goes into a rapid turn to the right. Several naval officers appear from nowhere. They are viewing the sea to the starboard side with binoculars. The music has stopped. The man with the accordion is seated on deck with the accordion lying on his lap. Some of the women are down on their knees hugging their small children. I look to the front of the ship and see that a minesweeper has stopped at a distance to our right. The ship is picking up speed, and at the same time, it swerves without warning to the left and continues in that direction. I approach a group of women and children now surrounding an officer. He is gesturing to the rear of the ship. He explains that a Russian submarine fired a torpedo at us. But it missed its target. The ship will be heading east to get closer to shore, and then, will continue south when it is closer to land. He tells the group that in a short while, we will see the Latvian shoreline. He quickly leaves the group, ascends a flight of stairs, and disappears.

I walk over to the left side of the ship and stand there, staring into the distance. The accordion player is now leaning against the side where I am standing. I look back, and everyone is gone. Only the man and I are still there on the open deck. I see the minesweeper passing the

Moltkefels in the distance, and in a short while, it is again to our front. I sense the ship slowly changing its course to the right. I'm confused about the direction the ship is taking. But I stay and keep staring into the distance. The accordion player is to my left. He yells the word, "Maa!" It is the Estonian word for land.

I see a faint dark line in the distance. After a while I can see colors, mostly green, appear in place of the dark line I saw at first. In a little while, I begin to see small houses dotting the shoreline. The Moltkefels now seems to be turning south, because the shoreline does not get any closer. To me it is very comforting to have this sight of land instead of the open sea to all sides.

Word of this sighting has reached the ship's hold, and women, with their children, are now crowding the side of the ship where land can be seen. Some pick up their children and cradle them in their arms, pointing in the direction of the land. My mother and sister appear near me, and I point out the shoreline to them. Somehow I feel very much like an adult because I was one of the first to see land—along with the accordion player.

He again begins to play as he stands with his back to the side of the ship. The women with their children are speaking aloud. The sight of the land has brought some comfort and security into our fast-changing lives.

I keep looking at the land and think that perhaps we will be on land soon, though certainly not in Germany, which is our destination. The day passes, and as the ship moves on with the minesweeper in front, I have time to think about what was—and what lies ahead. I'm no longer worried about the airplane overhead or the submarine, and when night falls, I crawl onto the bed where my mother and sister are already asleep. I feel some hunger, because up to this point, I've only eaten some bread and thin soup and a bite of the ham in my backpack. But I fall asleep, ignoring the empty, hungry feelings.

I am awakened by silence. The ship seems to be quiet. It is not rising and dropping as it was before. There is no noise or vibration from the engines. Instantly, I know that we are standing still.

Chapter 25.

RIGA HARBOR, LATVIA AND LOADING OF HORSES AND RUSSIAN PRISONERS

I get up and walk out to the deck. It is barely daylight, and to my right, I see buildings. I walk to one side of the ship and notice that a gangplank is down, resting on the concrete pier. A mass of grey figures is seated on the ground. There seem to be hundreds of the seated men, surrounded by soldiers with rifles. Beyond them, I see freight cars with their doors closed. I ask a sailor near me where we are. He says we are at the Riga harbor, in Latvia, and will be taking on several hundred Russian prisoners and horses.

I stay on the side of the ship where I can observe some activity near the freight cars. Soldiers are opening the freight cars' doors and leading horses down a plank. As a horse is led closer to the ship, soldiers wrap a large piece of heavy netting around its body. The netting is then attached to a hook and cable which leads to an overhead crane.

The horse is stumbling in an effort to gain some balance as the crane begins to lift it. Within seconds, the horse is airborne above the deck of the ship, and the crane swings the horse over the deck and down into a large opening leading to a hold. In a short time, the net appears from the hold, swings around and down again, where soldiers are ready to attach the next horse.

I approach a sailor who is also watching the loading of horses, and I ask him where the horses are going. He tells me that these horses are coming from the Eastern Front, and most are sick or injured. He tells me that they will be killed once in Germany, and their hooves will be processed into glue, and the meat will be canned and rationed for food.

I settle along the side of the ship and continue to watch the loading. As I watch, my concentration is interrupted by accordion music coming from the middle of the deck.

The music is very slow and sorrowful, and suddenly I feel sad. My thoughts are no longer back in the comfort of my grandparents' farm, or the future, and what it might bring. Rather, I now think of what is happening at the moment. Such as a feeling of hunger, which is something I have not experienced before. I keep looking over the side of the ship, and I move closer to the area where the horses are being loaded. A large, brown horse is being loaded. As the crane lifts the horse on its way to the ship's hold, I look at him, and our eyes meet. The horse looks sad, and he reminds me of one of my grandparents' horses.

My thoughts drift again to the farm where I was happy. Now everything has changed, and I still wish we could have stayed and not left for the unknown. But I am not bored.

As I look to the rear of the ship, I see that a gangplank has been lowered. The soldiers surrounding the Russian prisoners order them to get up from where they have been sitting. As they struggle to their feet, some fall down, then get up on their knees and try to get up again. Some of the German guards become impatient, yelling orders in German, instructing the prisoners to move and get going. A line of prisoners has reached the bottom of the gangplank, and they are beginning to ascend the steep climb to the deck above.

Although none of the prisoners is carrying anything except the tattered uniforms covering their thin bodies, they are struggling under their own weight. Some fall. And if they are lucky, they have a stronger prisoner behind them who tries to lift them to their feet. In this way, they reach the deck. They are directed to the rear of the ship, where they drop into a sitting position. I see one prisoner drop to his knees at the bottom of the gangplank. Rather than try to get up, he crawls on his hands and knees to the top and continues in this manner to the rear, where he joins his fellow prisoners who have already arrived.

As I watch the loading of this human cargo, I move closer to the gangplank. My thoughts drift back to the Tuule Farm, where during 1943 and 1944, the German army assigned Maxim, a Russian prisoner, to work on my grandparents' farm. I remember that he was a very friendly man, always smiling. He helped with all the farm tasks, and on Sundays, insisted that he take the cows and sheep to the pasture surrounded by the forest. He did this gladly, and I was happy to have one day without any shepherding tasks. I begin to look at the faces of the ascending prisoners, thinking that perhaps Maxim is among them. But I don't see him among the tired-looking men slowly stepping, and sometimes crawling, up the long, steep gangplank.

My mother and sister appear. My mother tells me that our plans have changed. She had hoped to find her distant relative, who lives near Berlin, after our arrival in Germany. But an officer on the ship has told her that we should go as far into Germany as possible, because the Eastern Front is approaching fast. We must continue to flee as far from the Front as possible, because Germany is losing the war. I know this means we will be even further from home. I try not to think about it, because it makes me want to cry, and I know I cannot let this happen, because I am too old to show such emotion. Especially, since I am in charge of our only possessions— a backpack and two suitcases.

I glance back at the pier and notice that the horses, as well as the prisoners, have all been loaded onto the ship. The area in the harbor where they were is empty now, except for a group of German soldiers gathered in a circle, smoking cigarettes and laughing. A German staff car pulls up to the gangplank that the Russian prisoners have just climbed. Two German naval officers exit the car and immediately run up the gangplank. As they reach the deck, sailors begin winching up the gangplank.

Chapter 26.

OVER ROUGH SEAS TO DANZIG WITH THE ONE-LEGGED ACCORDION PLAYER

As soon as the gangplank is removed, the ship's whistle blows, and men in the harbor unhook the massive ropes from posts that have held the ship in place. The heavy ropes are dragged onto the ship's deck, the ship vibrates, and the engines are engaged. I run to the other side of the ship and see tugboats starting to pull the ship from the dock, and before I realize it, we are clear of the pier.

I again hear accordion music coming from across the deck. The one-legged accordion player, leaning against a solid container, is playing a slow, haunting tune. With this background of music, I see the friendly Riga harbor slowly moving into the distance. We are going into the unknown once more, and I can't help but think of what may lie ahead. Will there be more Russian submarines and bombers overhead? Whatever dangers will lurk in the Baltic, as the Moltkefels continues her journey to Germany?

The ship's loudspeaker comes to life, announcing that the evening meal will be served in about half-an-hour. I walk into the ship's hold where my mother and sister are sitting on the edge of the bunk. I pick up my tin container and my spoon and tell them that I am going to go outside and get in line for food. They both follow me, with my mother carrying their utensils. My sister follows last, and we get in the line, which already extends across the deck.

As we walk past the servers, I extend my arm over the steaming kettle, and a sailor fills my bowl to the brim. The next man hands me a slice of bread, and we move on. I decide to stay on the deck, but my mother and sister return to the ship's hold. As I sip my soup directly from the bowl, I see the Latvian coastline slowly disappearing to our left.

After I drink the thin soup, I take my spoon, scrape up the few pieces of potato and carrot, and spread the mix on my bread. I fold the piece of rye and slowly eat it, trying to make it last as long as possible. I wash the cup and spoon in a large container holding water that has a mild smell of soap.

As I head toward the ship's hold, I glance up and notice that all the lights on deck and above are off as the night is approaching. In the hold, I see a faint ceiling light in the distance. My mother and sister are already lying down and asleep in our bunk. I lie down near the edge and hear soft voices coming from different directions. A child cries nearby. I close my eyes and fall asleep.

In the morning, I wake up and feel the ship swaying. All around me, I hear children crying. There are hundreds of women and children in the hold, and someone is howling. My mother is cradling my sister in her arms, while seated at the edge of our bed. I tell my mother that I am going onto the deck, and she warns me to be careful.

On deck, I'm thrown off balance. I see the front of the ship rise, and a few moments later, it crashes downward with water spraying onto the deck. I sit on deck and look to both sides. I try to see some land, but all I see is water rising and dropping. I approach a sailor who is smoking a cigarette at the front of the ship. As he blows smoke from his mouth, it disappears quickly. I ask him when we will arrive in Germany. He says, "In another day and night" and adds, "only if the ship doesn't run into trouble." I know what he means—only if we are not torpedoed by a submarine or sunk by a bomb dropped from a plane.

For some reason his remark does not bother me. I should be scared, but I am no longer afraid. I only think of the excitement that has lately filled my life. And I remember that I do not have to go to school.

I'm taken from my thoughts by an announcement that breakfast will be served. I go back to the ship's hold and tell my mother that it's time to eat. She tells me that she and my sister will not eat because they are seasick. As I leave them, I look around and see people bent over with one hand covering their mouth. They are throwing up, and I feel that I have to get out on deck before I also get sick—and have to spend the day lying down on the bunk, listening to the crying and howling, and smelling the vomit.

The deck is deserted except for a few women standing in line. As the food arrives, I notice that there is only dark bread, sliced. I step up, and the sailor who is serving tells me that I can have as many pieces as I want because many people are seasick and won't be eating. Only the evening meal will be served, he adds, as he hands me a stack of dark bread. He tells me to put the bread inside my shirt. I open the top buttons of my shirt and stuff the bread down the front, then button it up to prevent anyone seeing it. I think the sailor does not want to get in trouble for giving me too much.

I walk to the side of the ship, sit on a large metal box, and begin eating the dark bread. I wonder if this padlocked box is where they keep the life jackets for the passengers. As I look to the distance, beyond the side of the ship, I see nothing but high waves with white foam swirling around. I see no land or other ships. A feeling of boredom passes through me. I return to the hold, but the horrible smell of vomit and the screams of children drive me back on deck. I wish I had a book that I could read, and I almost welcome the sound of the planes overhead, with our anti-aircraft guns going into action.

Looking back at the opening to the ship's hold, I see the man with one leg, on crutches, trying to move and keep his balance. He motions with his hand in my direction, and I think he wants me to come to him. I move towards him as fast as I can, trying to keep my balance. As I get there, he asks me if I can help him walk. He tells me to stand at his back and put my hands around his waist. I do as I am told, and we begin a slow walk toward the metal container I was sitting on. As he moves his crutches ahead, I follow him slowly. He swings his only leg ahead of the crutches. We reach the container, and I help him sit down. He thanks me, and tells me that he had to leave the hold because the screaming children and smell of vomit have nearly caused him to get sick.

I ask him what happened to his leg, and he tells me that he was wounded on the Eastern Front a year ago, when he was hit by fragments from an artillery shell. He tells me that he is lucky because he only lost his leg. Many of the soldiers who were near him are dead and buried somewhere in Russia. When he asks about me, I tell him about school and my grandparents' farm and about my father who stayed behind. He then looks at me, puts his hand on my shoulder, and tells me that he hopes that I will again, someday, see my father.

He then digs down into his pocket, takes out a pack of cigarettes, and lights one. He tells me that he would gladly give me a cigarette, but he thinks I am too young to smoke. We sit on the deck, occasionally talking about his parents who decided to stay behind, and he also hopes that, someday, he will see them again.

After a while, I tell the one-legged accordion player that I would like to walk toward the rear of the ship to see the Russian prisoners. I ask him if he would like to go along, but he tells me that he will stay and wait. He tells me to be careful. I walk slowly around the center structure of the ship and stop at a long wire gate. Beyond it, I see the prisoners huddled together, some sitting and some lying on the deck. There are several guards surrounding the mass of people, but I also see several guards walking among the prisoners handing out large pieces of rye bread. As a sailor with a basket approaches a group of prisoners I see many thin, white hands reaching up to him. Some of the prisoners lying on the deck also reach upward, and as soon as a prisoner grasps a piece of bread, I see his hand go to his mouth, and the bread disappears. Some of the stronger prisoners get up, and one by one, stumble to the huge water container, where they fill a tin cup hanging on the container and empty it into their mouths. I look for Maxim again, but I do not see him.

After a while, I return to the front of the ship and join the one-legged accordion player, who is still seated where I left him. I look around and see no other boys my age. This makes me feel good, because I actually feel much older. I speak to adults, and I am seated next to a man who has been in war, and he talks to me as though I am his age. I feel, from here on, my mother can no longer see me as a child. I feel much more confident about our situation as we head into the unknown. Somehow, I feel safe and have no fear.

My thoughts are interrupted by the accordion player's voice. He asks me if I would go into the ship's hold and bring him the accordion. He describes its location, which is way at the far side of the hold, toward the right. As I enter the hold, I hear children crying and a horrible smell is everywhere. It almost causes me to get sick myself, as I feel a strange rolling inside my stomach. I run to the other side of the hold and see the accordion. I get it, put the straps around my shoulders, and hurriedly walk to the opposite side. As I pass near my mother and sister, I notice that both are asleep. This is good, because I do not have to explain why I am not with them.

I walk quickly to the one-legged man, and as I stand in front of him, he removes the straps from my shoulders, turns the accordion around, and places it on his lap. He remains seated, runs his fingers up and down the keyboards on both sides, and after having done this, thanks me for bringing his accordion.

Before I have a chance to sit down, the man begins to play a slow tune that somehow blends with the rocking of the ship. A few sailors gather around us, and I can see they seem relaxed as they light their cigarettes. The smoke they blow into the air is captured by the strong wind, and it disappears in small clouds.

I feel good, because I did bring the one-legged man's accordion to him. I feel I am part of the music he is creating. I sit on the deck with my back to the metal box. I feel tired, and I doze off to sleep.

I awaken to an announcement on the ship's loudspeaker. I miss the message, but I notice sailors bringing in containers of steaming soup and containers of bread. As I get up, I notice the accordion player asleep, sitting on deck, his back to the steel box, his accordion cradled on his lap and his head resting on the accordion.

I decide to see whether my mother and sister are ready to eat. I enter the hold, see that both are asleep, and decide not to awaken them. Instead, I retrieve my tin container and return to the deck. I get in line, and as I pass through, a sailor fills my cup with soup and hands me two slices of rye bread. I sit next to the accordion player, and he opens his eyes and looks over at me. He asks me if I could bring him some soup and bread. I place my cup of soup on the deck, take his cup, and get his food. He thanks me and begins to eat by dipping a slice of bread into the steaming soup, then eating the soup-soaked slice very slowly. I do the same, and again, experience a feeling that I am somehow part of his music.

After he finishes eating his soup and bread, he asks me to pick up his accordion. I help him fasten the straps over his shoulders, and as soon as this is done, he runs his fingers over the keys and begins to play a fast tune. He gets an immediate audience as sailors appear. They light their cigarettes and begin to tap their feet on the deck.

The music seems to put everyone in a good mood, and I forget the war and the danger that seems to surround the ship. I try not to think about anything beyond the ship, because whenever I think back on my life, I get a feeling of sadness. I avoid thinking of my grandparents and my father. It seems as though these things are no longer part of my life. Everything seems to have faded from my memory, and I seem to only think of what is happening now. I don't even think of what lies ahead.

The accordion player has quit playing, and he asks me to carry the accordion to his bunk. I hang the instrument over my shoulders and start walking. Behind me, he takes long steps with the help of his crutches. When we get to his bunk, I lay the accordion on it. He tells me that he is tired, and lies down.

I return to my mother and sister, who are seated on the edge of the bunk. I lie down and promptly fall asleep. Only to be awakened by an announcement the next morning, saying, "Food is served." My mother and sister decide to get in line, and we are served soup and slices of black bread. We return to the bunk and eat the food. I ask my mother for some ham, but she tells me that we have to save it, because once we land in Danzig we will have to furnish our own food to our final destination. I try to find out where we are going after landing. She tells me we will not know until we arrive. I decide to go to sleep. I place my backpack under my head, and promptly fall asleep.

Chapter 27.

ARRIVING IN DANZIG, GERMANY AND THE JOURNEY TO BERLIN

I am awakened by an announcement on the loudspeaker. I can't quite understand it because of the noise, but my mother and sister are seated on the edge of the bunk. We are no longer moving. My mother tells me that we have arrived in Danzig and that we should gather our belongings and go on deck. I place the backpack over my shoulders and grab the two suitcases. I don't have to get dressed, because I have been wearing the same double-layered clothing ever since we left Tallinn several days ago, when I lost track of time.

As I emerge from the hold, I am blinded by sunlight. The ship has docked, and I realize that I have slept through our last night of travel over the Baltic. I look into the distance, and I see buildings reflecting the early morning sun. I feel good that the most difficult part of our journey is over, but I also think of the place we left, and realize that with every passing moment, the distance to our home is becoming greater.

What started as a journey on a horse and wagon, with my grandfather driving as we left the Tuule Farm—followed by a ride on an open truck loaded with women and children, their baggage, and an empty coffin—has led across the Baltic Sea to Danzig, by way of the Moltkefels. As we approach the steep gangplank and a descent off the ship, it seems there is no longer a return to the place I left behind.

Before I know it, I am standing on the dock of Danzig harbor. My mother is leading my sister by her hand, to a group of women wearing grey uniforms. She speaks to one of them, and the woman directs us to a small group gathered nearby. As we join them, we are told that our next destination will be Berlin. However, we will not leave until evening. Now we must wait.

In the late afternoon, a freight train stops near where we are gathered and sitting on the side of the track. We are told to climb onto the box cars with their large doors open. We do as told, hauling up our possessions—the backpack, two suitcases, and my mother's small red case. Two soldiers walk back and forth along the train and make sure that everyone is on board.

There are about thirty people in the car that my mother, my sister, and I have climbed into. I decide to sit on the edge of the door, and one of the soldiers warns me to move further in when the train leaves. He tells me that when the train picks up speed, I could easily fall out. I am very bored and would rather wander around the harbor. But the thought of the train suddenly leaving without me keeps me from jumping off.

My mother has opened the large container of lard that one of us was carrying. We all sit around the container, scoop lard onto slices of dried bread, and begin to eat. I am not very hungry, but my mother tells me to eat, because once the train leaves, it will be difficult to eat in the dark.

After eating one slice of bread with lard, I tell my mother that I am not hungry. I decide to jump off the train, but as soon as my feet hit the ground, I see a soldier about two boxcars away, pointing a finger in my direction, then motioning his hand toward the boxcar. I know immediately what he is saying, and I quickly climb back into the car, turn around, and sit down with my legs hanging over the opening. He again looks in my direction but makes no gestures with his hand. I assume that he is happy that I obeyed his first order.

The crying of children in the boxcar has become unbearable. I think of my own childhood, and I can't remember ever crying. A thought comes to me—as a child I often had earaches, and my mother would pour a sticky yellow liquid on a piece of cotton, then push a piece into each ear. It seemed to help the pain, and it also helped block out things my mother said. I know that we have no cotton with us, but another thought comes to me. I will have to find something that can be forced into my ears. I take out my pocketknife and cut a small piece of cloth off my outer shirt. Then I tear it into two small pieces and force one into each ear, making sure that a loose end is not hanging out. As soon as I complete this task, there is silence. I lie back on the floor of the boxcar and close my eyes.

I am awakened by a sudden shaking of the boxcar. I sit up and see trees moving slowly past. Finally, the train has started. Our journey into the unknown is continuing.

I get up and find the large sliding door partially open. I again become aware of children crying, in spite of my plugged ears. I can't escape this noise, as I did on the ship. I see that my mother and sister are sleeping with their bodies propped against some luggage. I go to the door and sit down with my legs hanging out the door.

The train has picked up speed, and with darkness approaching, the passing objects have become shadowy figures. Occasionally, I see a house with a light in a window, and I wonder what it's like to be inside a house, seated around a table, eating a meal that has been cooked. I wonder if we will ever again be in a house, or will we always be riding in a ship's hold or in a railroad car. The only comforting thought is that, if I were home, the time to start school would be fast approaching.

My mother's voice interrupts my thoughts. Because the moving train is making noise with the clatter created by the wheels only a few feet from where I am, I pretend not to hear her. I hope that I can ignore her, because I do not want to leave the doorway and return to the crying babies. A short time later, I feel a hand on my shoulder. I look around, and it is my mother. She tells me to come into the freight car and eat something. I get up, turn around, and join my mother and sister.

My mother hands me a slice of dried rye bread and tells me to make a sandwich by spreading on lard which has some fried bacon and onion pieces. I follow her order and quickly devour the sandwich. I am not really hungry, but the meal tastes good. I decide to have another slice. I see my sister slowly eating a slice prepared by our mother. She looks up at me, and I see a smile on her face, illuminated by a small candle that someone near us has just lighted. I have not seen my sister smile in a long time—perhaps not since we left Piirita to board the Moltkefels for our journey to Germany. It is good to see her smile.

I think of times when we would walk through fields of daisies behind our home in Viljandi and she would pick a flower, hand it to me, and smile.

But my thoughts quickly return to the crowded freight car. Since it is dark outside, I decide to lie down. I place my head against my backpack. The movement of the train, with occasional swaying of the boxcar, creates a feeling of tiredness, and I drift off to sleep.

I don't know how long I have slept, but I am awakened by a commotion of people milling around the large sliding door which is now wide open. It is light outside. I feel no motion of the train, and I quickly approach the open door. I see people getting off, and a soldier nearby tells us to get off and go to a long table.

My mother and sister follow me to the table, where I see piles of sliced rye bread. A woman motions to us to come nearer. As we arrive at the table, we are handed a thick slice of bread and an empty tin cup. There are two large containers at the end of the table. A woman bends down, fills a ladle, and pours water into my cup. We are told to eat the bread, drink the water, and return the cup. The woman fills the cup again with water, then looks at my sister and says, "She has such beautiful blond hair." She takes the cup from my sister, empties it, and ladles milk out of the other container for my sister. My mother thanks the woman, and we move on to eat the meal of bread and water.

Before long, we are told to get on the freight car again, and once the platform is empty, the train begins to move. I return to my spot on the floor and notice that my mother and sister are already curled up, ready to sleep. I decide to do the same, and before long I, too, fall asleep.

When I awaken, the train has stopped. The door is open. I see people standing on the platform, but somehow they look different. They do not carry bags and crying children in their arms. I think they must live here.

I get up and jump onto the platform. As I look around, I see a man in uniform. I ask him where we are, and he says, "You are in the main train station of Berlin."

I quickly return to the boxcar and tell my mother. She is up and gathering all our belongings. I strap on the backpack and grab the two suitcases and get off the train. My mother and sister follow me. As we reach the platform, a man in the crowd announces that all the refugees who have arrived from Danzig should remain where they are and await instructions.

Certain destinations to the West are announced. My mother tells me to stay with my sister. She approaches a woman wearing a uniform. They speak briefly, and she returns. She tells me that we have been assigned to go to a small town called Graitschen, near Jena. I am thankful, because I am sick and tired of wearing double-layered clothing and listening to crying babies. But I do not say this aloud.

Chapter 28.

LEAVING BERLIN AND THE JOURNEY TO JENA AND GRAITSCHEN

A loudspeaker comes on, and we are instructed to board a train. We hurry to follow instructions, because there is a long line forming. There is a great crowd of people and they all want a seat on the train. My mother quickly tells me to climb onto a car through an open window. She supports me from behind, as I grab ahold of the windowsill. I pull myself up and roll into the car. She quickly hands me our luggage and tells me to put our bags on a seat in the compartment and help to lift in my sister. As my mother lifts her, I grab ahold of her arms and pull her up. I tell her to sit down on a seat, and when I look out my mother has already joined the waiting line of passengers.

After a short wait, she boards the train and joins us. The compartment is crowded by now, but we have two seats. My mother sits down and holds my sister on her lap. I take the seat next to her after I shove our bags under the seat. I look out the open window and see that everyone has boarded the train. In a moment, air raid sirens begin to howl. The train moves forward, enters a tunnel, and stops. We are lucky to have this tunnel as an air raid shelter. I realize that the danger from the air has followed us from the Moltkefels.

As we wait for the danger to be over, my thoughts turn to my grandparents' farm and the time when my grandmother told me a story about seeing butterflies in the spring. She told me that if the first butterfly that I see in the spring is black, I will die before next spring arrives. However, if the first butterfly is light colored, I will not die before the following spring. I try to think back to last spring, trying to recall the color of the butterfly I first saw, and I remember that it was white. This fact seems to make the fear of bombs leave me, and as I think of our present situation on this train going to Jena, the train begins to move.

We emerge from the dark tunnel and enter the outside. It's filled with sunshine, and a cloudless sky. I think that maybe all the danger we have experienced is behind us, on the other side of the dark tunnel. As I look at the passing countryside of green fields and forests, I become tired and soon fall asleep.

I'm awakened by crying children. I find the pieces of my shirt in my pants pocket and stuff a piece in each ear. My mother asks me why I am doing this, and I tell her that I am getting earaches, and the pieces of cloth stuffed in each ear help the pain. She asks me where I got the pieces of cloth, and I tell her that I found a piece of cloth in Danzig harbor, lying on the ground, and saved it. I am very careful not to tell my mother that I cut the pieces off the bottom part of my shirt. I know she would become angry because I have damaged one of the two shirts that I own and am now wearing under my coat.

The train is moving at a fast pace, and I look out the window and catch sight of a small house in the distance, partly hidden by trees. I see smoke rising from a chimney. It rises straight into the blue sky. As the house fades into the distance, I remember another story that my grandmother told me when I was staying at Tuule Farm. She said that when we see smoke coming from a chimney in the morning, and it blows down or sideways, it's going to be a day without happiness. But when the smoke comes out straight and goes toward the sky, we will have a lucky day. With this thought, I am again rocked to sleep by the movement of the train.

I don't know how long I have slept, but I am awakened by a strong jolt as the train comes to a stop. I look out the window, and see a line of women in uniforms standing over a table filled with slices of dark bread and steaming kettles. I tell my mother that I am getting off the train, and she tells me that she will follow shortly with my sister. I hurry into a line which is forming fast, and when I reach the table a woman asks, "Flüchtling?" I know she is asking if I am escaping from somewhere. I say, "Ja." and nod my head. She then hands me two slices of bread and the next server hands me a tin cup filled with a steaming liquid. I thank her and move away to sit on the platform, with my back against a pillar. I look into the cup, and it is filled with a brown liquid and small pieces of cabbage leaves. I take a piece of rye bread, break it in half, and dip it into the cabbage soup. As I place it in my mouth, I feel a warm, pleasant taste. And as I swallow the soup-soaked bread, I become very hungry, and slowly drink the soup, and then eat the bread. As I stay seated, I see my mother and sister walking through the line of food.

I sit there holding the empty cup. A woman in a grey uniform approaches me, carrying a steaming ladle. She stands over me and empties the ladle into my empty cup. I thank her, and before she turns to leave, she kneels down in front of me and gently touches one of my cheeks with her free hand. I try to say something, but words do not seem to come out. And before I know it, she gets up, and she is gone. I continue to sip my soup very slowly, because I am trying to make it last for a long time.

My mother and sister join me, and my sister sits down next to me, resting her back against my side. I tell her to soak her bread in the soup, and she does. My mother is standing over us, and tells us to hurry because the train will be leaving shortly, and we must follow her instructions. In a short time, the food is gone. I get up, and take my sister's hand, and help her get up, and we walk to the serving tables to return our cups to the women wearing uniforms. One of the women looks at my sister, and turning to the woman next to her, points her finger at my sister and tells the woman, "She is so Aryan." The other woman looks at my sister, nods her head, and smiles in agreement. I think it must be good to be Aryan. But I don't know what it means.

After this brief stop, we return to the train. We barely sit down when the train begins to move. I close my eyes but cannot fall asleep. I start looking at the passing countryside, which drifts by slowly, because the train does not seem to gather any speed. I start to wonder if we will reach our destination at night, which would mean that after getting off the train, we would probably have to sleep outside again—and could not take off our double-layered clothing, which we have been wearing now for at least ten days.

I am getting very, very tired of the crying children around me. In spite of the pieces of my shirt stuffed in my ears, the noise seems to be louder and never stops. I am beginning to hate small children and babies that have surrounded me ever since we left Tallinn on the Moltkefels— which seems like forever. I cover my ears with my hands and fall asleep.

I don't know how long I have slept, but the train has stopped. It is daylight, and I see a town and people walking on the train station platform. The sign says Jena.

A woman in a grey uniform has a band on her arm with a red cross on it. She enters the car and announces that all the refugees destined to go to Graitschen should get off. My mother quickly opens the window near our seats— and tells me to climb through and follow her instructions. The moment I hit the platform, she begins to hand me our bags and the backpack. And when this is done, she tells me not to leave the bags. I follow her instructions. And soon I see her emerge from the train, leading my sister by her hand.

The woman in the grey uniform tells us not to leave the area, and then quickly returns to the train, which starts to move. Two men in uniform approach our group, and one of them tells us to take our bags and get onto their nearby truck. They help some of the women get on and before long we are on a road, leaving the station and Jena behind. The open truck travels down a road lined with apple trees which have red fruit hanging from the branches. After a ride that seems to pass quickly, we come to a small village. The truck stops in front of a building with a sign saying, *Gasthaus*. It is a tavern. In front of the entrance, there are several men and women. All looking at us. One of the drivers tells us that we are in Graitschen. It is about noontime.

Chapter 29.

HERR MÜLLER'S FARM IN GRAITSCHEN

We get off the truck and gather our belongings near the tavern. A man emerges from the tavern and invites us to come in. He explains that we will be placed in homes throughout the village, and we should wait for instructions.

Soon a woman walks out of the tavern and waves in our direction, motioning toward the door. We enter the tavern. My mother and sister walk toward the counter, which has a man behind it. There are rows of glasses on the top of the counter. My mother opens a small bag that she has been carrying and puts several paper bills on the counter. The man behind the row of glasses picks up a glass and fills it with a foaming light brown liquid and places it in front of her. He then looks at my sister and me, and my mother says something to him. He pours a red liquid from a glass container and gives it to my mother, who then gives it to my sister, who immediately drinks it, and begins to smile.

The man then looks at me, and I point at the foamy glass. He looks in the direction of my mother, who nods her head, and he picks up a small glass, fills it from a spout on the counter, and hands it to me. I grasp the glass with both hands and bring it to my lips. As I slowly drink the foamy light brown liquid, it reminds me of the liquid that I used to drink out of the barrel at the Tuule Farm. My grandfather's homemade brew. This liquid is sweeter, and as I slowly allow it to go down my throat, I feel good. And happy. The man behind the counter picks up the money and walks to a group of women near us. They motion toward the spout which says Bier, and they all ask for what sounds like beer.

I join my mother and sister at a table and continue to slowly drink the beer. After a few sips, and feeling happy, I let my thoughts return to the Tuule Farm, and the memories bring back good moments.

My thoughts are interrupted by a group of men entering the tavern. One of them speaks to the group of refugees. He says that we will be living on farms, and we will be working, due to the shortage of workers because of the war. A tall, thin man approaches my mother, and they begin to speak. After a few minutes, my mother tells me that this is Herr Müller, and we will be living on Herr Müller's farm and helping him. I quickly empty my glass of beer, gather our belongings, and we follow Herr Müller as he leaves the tavern.

We follow him down a narrow street and soon arrive at a group of buildings surrounded by a stone fence. After going through the gate and the large yard, we enter the house, where we are introduced to his wife, the grandmother, and the two sons, who seem older than I am. After a short conversation between my mother and the Müllers, we leave the kitchen and follow the farmer's wife, Frau Müller, outside. We walk toward an attached stone building next to the barn and are led upstairs, and down a short hallway, to a storage room. The room has a coal-burning stove, a table, several wood chairs, and some narrow beds which are covered by fluffy blankets. Frau Müller talks to my mother for a while, explaining the stove, and then motions for us to follow her back to the hallway, where she shows us the toilet room. She then tells us that we should unpack, and she will return later.

I unpack my backpack and place everything on a bed. My mother tells me to change the clothing that I have been wearing for what seems forever, because I have lost track of time. I am relieved to find a change of clothing, and take it into the toilet room. I try to wash in a small metal pail, which I fill with cold water from the faucet. There is no sink. After I am done, I thankfully put on the clean clothing from my backpack. I am left with a pile of dirty clothing. I empty the pail into the toilet and return everything to our room. My mother tells me to place everything under my bed, and wait for her and my sister, while they use the toilet room.

Shortly after they return, there is a knock on the door, and Frau Müller lets herself in. She invites us for the evening meal. She leads us into the yard and tells us that if we hear any air raid sirens we should immediately leave our room and go into the basement. She shows us the cellar door entrance into the basement shelter. She then leads us into their house, and their large kitchen.

The kitchen table is filled with food. Sausage in slices, rye bread, and a steaming kettle of soup. It smells very good, like the Tuule Farm kitchen. The grandmother, with a friendly smile on her face, and the two boys, are also there. Frau Müller introduces everyone again. The boys are Heinz and Heinrich. I can't wait to eat.

Frau Müller fills our bowls with a meat and vegetable soup, and we begin to eat. My mother tells me to eat slowly, and wait for others, but I'm looking at food that I have not seen in such quantity for what seems a long time. The fact that I am eating very fast seems to please the Müllers.

Herr Müller tells my mother, between bites of food, what she has to do tomorrow. First is to get food ration cards somewhere in the village, along with a Fremdenpass, or Foreigner's Pass, which will give us the official status of refugees. He also says that my mother and I will be asked to help with house and farm work. Then he looks at me and tells me I will be expected to attend a local school. I am not very happy with this, and try to explain I would rather help on the farm. But he is not satisfied with this idea. He tells me I must go to school in a few days and that I will like the school, because I will be studying in German—and this will be good.

After we have finished the main meal, the grandmother brings out a huge flat cake, layered with cuts of plums and covered with a white cream. I have never seen a cake this big. I finish a piece immediately, because it is so good. The grandmother, smiling, hands me another.

After finishing the food, we all remain at the table, as the grandmother begins to clean the dishes. Herr Müller asks my mother about my father. She tells him that he had to remain behind because men over the age of sixteen could not leave Estonia. At this point, Herr Müller opens a bottle of red wine and fills everyone's glass, except my sister's. She is given a glass full of red liquid that reminds me of a fruit drink. We all slowly sip the sweet wine, and as I feel the warm wine passing down my throat, I feel even better.

When the wine is gone, my mother thanks the Müllers for providing us with a place to live and for a good meal. My sister and I, also, thank them, and then we three return to our room, which is now our new home.

I look at my bed, which is covered with a fluffy blanket. When I fold it back, I notice a bird's feather coming out of it. I show the feather to my mother, and she explains that the blanket is filled with goose feathers and is very warm. She adds that when the weather becomes cold in winter, it will keep me warm, even if there is very little heat in the room.

My sister is playing with a small stuffed dog which was given to her by our cousin Valdo, who is now somewhere on the Eastern Front. I hope he is safe.

My mother begins to write a letter. I ask her who she is writing to, and she says it is to her relative who lives near Berlin. She is the one we were going to live with. My mother is letting her know our new location, because if my father reaches Germany, he will undoubtedly go to her house, expecting to find us. This relative can then tell him where we are now, and hopefully, he will reach this place called Graitschen.

The memory of my father seems to be fading, along with the tearful good-bye at Tallinn Harbor, when the Moltkefels blew her loud whistle on a sunny late afternoon to signal our departure. Although it has been less than two weeks—it seems like forever.

I am getting very tired, and after taking off my shirt and pants, I slip under the soft blanket, and quickly fall asleep.

I'm awakened by a loud siren. My mother is shaking me, and she tells me to go into the basement. I dress on my way out the door. She is ahead of me, carrying my sister. As we enter the yard, I see Herr Müller standing, looking into the sky. He is wearing a strange, round metal helmet, which has a long sharp-tipped piece on the top. When I ask about it, he says it is from World War I. We quickly go down the stairs into the basement. The Müller family, including the grandmother, is already there, seated on benches. I see a pile of potatoes in the corner of the basement, and while I am looking at it, Frau Müller tells us that we can sit on the potatoes. I follow her invitation and sit down. My mother, still holding my sister, sits down next to me. There is complete silence around us.

Before long, I hear another siren. Herr Müller enters the basement and explains to my mother that the second siren indicates that a threat from the air is over, the planes are gone, and we can return to our room. I ask him where the planes are from, and he tells me that they are American and English planes and that they fly from airfields in England. He also explains that nighttime raids are frequent, but that they also happen during the daytime. At this, he wishes us a *gute Nacht*, or goodnight, with a faint smile, and we return to our room.

I decide to leave my clothes on when crawling into bed, because Herr Müller, while we were in the basement, told my mother that sometimes air raids occur more than once a night. With this thought, I fall asleep, again.

When I awaken, the room is filled with bright sunshine. My mother and sister are not in the room, and I am surprised that their leaving did not awaken me. I decide to get out of bed, and I am happy that I am already dressed. In spite of the air raids, I feel good. I am not being rocked by waves on the Moltkefels or awakened frequently by the motion of the train—or made deaf by crying babies in a freight car. Nor do I have to wear doubles of my clothes. Things are getting better.

I leave our room and go into the large yard. The Müller's yard is surrounded by their stone farm buildings, with a gate opening to the main road. The gate opening is quite wide, and I think this allows the farmer, Herr Müller, to move wagons out the gate, drawn by a tractor, or horses, or even cattle. Out on the street, I walk to my right, and a short distance ahead, I see the friendly tavern where I drank a beer yesterday.

When I walk to my left, I quickly come to a small stream to my right. I walk on, and see a bridge crossing the stream, and on the other side, I see a building which to me looks like a school, because there are children standing around in an open area. Some walk in twos, back and forth, at a rapid pace. I assume these are students, getting their exercise.

The thought of school bores me. I have not attended school since last spring, in Estonia, and I would much prefer to work for Herr Müller, rather than be forced to spend endless days in a school.

I turn around and quickly continue walking to the outskirts of the village. I now see that the farm houses and their buildings are part of the village. Farmers live side by side, with gates leading to their farm yards from the street. And all the farmers' fields actually circle the village. It is not like the farms in Estonia that stand by themselves, surrounded by their fields and forests, with neighbors sometimes a kilometer, or more, away. I can see the street is also lined with houses where people who are not farmers live. Everything looks very neat. It seems nice that a farmer can walk out his gate and be at the tavern without having to travel a long distance. I think my grandfather would like this. He would not have to make his own homemade brew, because the tavern would be close by. And he could take me with him.

I circle back to the Müller farm. As I enter the upstairs room, I see my mother and sister bent over the table unpacking items from my backpack. My mother explains that they have been to a Government Office to get her Fremdenpass, which shows her status as a refugee. She also has received ration cards, letting her buy certain food items once a week from local stores. She says that she used my backpack for shopping and lays out the items she has bought. There are three loaves of rye bread, a small package of margarine, several cans of meat, a bag of potatoes, a bag of flour, and then sugar and salt. Last she takes out a package wrapped with newspaper. When she opens it, I see that it contains a large pile of white flakes. She explains that these are crushed oat seeds, and they can be cooked in water and then eaten at any time.

I am getting bored and decide to sleep. My mother doesn't seem to object, and I quickly fall asleep—only to be awakened by sirens. My mother and sister are on their way out the door, and I follow them. It's a bright, sunny day, still warm. I look to the sky and hope to see planes overhead, but there are none. As we enter the basement, the Müllers are already seated. Herr Müller approaches and tells me I will be going to school, and he will take me to school in a few days. I tell him that I know where the school is because I have already walked there. He says he is glad I am anxious to start school. He also tells me I speak enough German to be able to get along. As our conversation ends, the sirens sound again, and we all exit the dark basement.

My mother tells me she wants us to walk to the tavern and get to know the village better, so we will know where the stores are. She adds that sometimes she expects me to go shopping for her.

When we enter the tavern, and approach the counter where the bartender stands, my mother asks for a beer, and the man fills a large glass. He then points at me, and my mother nods, but points at her glass midway down. The man then fills another glass, but only to the halfway mark.

My mother pays in paper money, and we all go to a table and sit down. I decide to drink my beer slowly. I bring the glass to my mouth, holding the glass with both hands, take a small sip, and swallow the light brown liquid. After I have consumed about half of my drink, I begin to feel happy and at ease. A woman comes to our table and puts a small glass of red liquid in front of my sister, who immediately begins to drink it. A smile enters her face. My mother tells her to drink slowly.

The woman and my mother begin to talk. My mother explains about our flight from the approaching Eastern Front—and the woman tells my mother that her brother has been on the Eastern Front with the

German army, and she hopes he will soon be home. But when I look at her, between sips from my glass, I can see she looks sad. This look of sadness seems to be on the faces of most people, ever since we left the Tuule Farm.

My mother's glass is now empty and the woman takes it to the man behind the counter, has it refilled, and returns it to our table. My mother gives her paper money, and the woman thanks her and returns to the place near the counter where the beer is kept. My glass is now empty, and my mother notices. She picks up her glass and pours some of her beer into mine. We remain seated for a long time, without speaking a word. I am beginning to realize that we rarely speak much, anymore.

My thoughts are interrupted by my mother touching my shoulder as she gets up from the table. She picks up the empty glasses, returns them to the counter, and as we walk to the door, I turn around and wave at the man behind the counter. He lifts his arm, waves, and smiles.

We enter the yard of the Müller house, and are greeted by Frau Müller. She tells my mother that I have to report to the local school. A man from the school stopped by and said I should arrive by eight in the morning on Monday, and my mother should accompany me.

I had hoped that since I am a refugee from the East, I would not be required to attend school. The worst, for me, is definitely happening, and I am not happy about it. But I realize there is very little I can do to change this burden. My mother seems to be happy about the news, and tells me I should like school—and study very hard.

Chapter 30.

SCHOOL STARTS IN GRAITSCHEN

After the weekend, my mother walks me to school. I'm assigned to a classroom full of boys my age. About twenty of them. The teacher tells the other students that I am a refugee from the East, and I am assigned a seat in the back row, which I like. My mother leaves, and class begins.

After about an hour, the teacher tells us that we can go outside for a break. We are lined up, and then we walk in pairs in a circle. This does not make much sense to me. In Viljandi, we were allowed to stand around in a school hallway and not expected to walk around in a circle. The German boys look at me with curiosity. They seem friendly, but nobody talks.

After about ten minutes, the teacher calls to us from the doorway, and the students closest to the door begin to enter the building, and we all follow. As we enter, another group of students begins to exit. They look a little older, but again, they are all boys. It occurs to me that this school is for boys only, and the girls must be going to another school. Just like in Estonia. My sister is not required to attend school for some reason. How fortunate for her.

Before we are seated, the teacher tells me that he would like to see me when school is dismissed for the day. I nod my head in agreement, and when school is dismissed, after what seems like forever, the teacher approaches me with an armful of books. He opens each book and explains to me what subject is discussed in each. There is German Grammar, Mathematics, History, Geography, and a book filled with stories. But there is not a Singing Class, like the one I had in Estonia. I will not miss the singing.

My teacher also informs me that since I am ten years old, I am assigned to a third-year level. He then asks me questions about earlier school, and I tell him, because of the war, I have only completed two years of school, but that I speak some German. He asks me about my family, and I describe my life in Viljandi and my grandparents' farm and the fact that we had to leave because the Russian army was approaching. He then tells me I should have no problem with school, because I understand him, and was able to answer his questions in German. He is friendly. He then tells me I can leave, but I should be back by eight in the morning the following day.

I gather my books, leave the school, and head back to the Müller's farmhouse. It is, perhaps, a short five-minute walk.

When I arrive for school the next day, the teacher approaches me and says that we are all required to participate in the Nazi salute. This means we must stand and raise our straightened right arm slightly above our shoulder. At the same time, we are to recite the Nazi pledge after the teacher. This begins the school day.

Next we are told to sit in our seats, and the class begins. Nobody misbehaves. Nobody talks unless called upon. And we always stand when we answer the teacher's questions—just like in Estonia. The school days go by. They are as long as in Viljandi and just as boring.

Later that first week, two boys in my class approach me after school and ask me where I came from. After I explain that we had to flee from Estonia as the Eastern Front approached and the Russians were coming closer, they tell me that they both have fathers on the Eastern Front and that they have not seen them for a long time. Nor have they heard from them. They both tell me they would like to see me after school, and then they can show me parts of the village and what surrounds it. They also say that, sometimes on Sundays, they like to walk to a nearby town called Bürgel, to the east, and they will take me along. As the conversation ends, we arrive at the Müller farm, and they say good-bye. I'm glad that I have met some other boys whom I can consider friends.

A few days later, my new friends ask me if I would like to walk to Bürgel after school. It is only about two kilometers by walking on the road, and even less, only about one kilometer, if we walk through fields and woods. After school that day, we set out on a road which is lined with apple trees. One of my friends tells me that we can eat the apples if they are on the ground. But it is not permissible to fill one's pockets and to take the apples home. I quickly find a large apple on the ground, but I notice that part of it is rotten. One of the boys hands me his pocketknife, and I cut out the brown soft spot. I bite into the apple, and the sweet warm flavor fills my mouth. I tell the boys that I have not eaten an apple since I left my grandparents' farm. They smile and tell me that I should walk every day on this road and eat apples.

We soon reach Bürgel. It is larger than Graitschen, and after wandering around streets, we head back. This time we walk through the fields and the woods. When I get back to the Müller's farm, my mother is very upset, for some reason. She says it is because I failed to tell her that I wasn't going to be home after school. I promise her that I will tell her in the future. I think some things never change.

Chapter 31.

LETTER FROM THE DISTANT RELATIVE AND A SHORTAGE OF FOOD

A few days later, a letter arrives from my mother's distant relative near Berlin. She writes that she has not heard from my father but hopes that it will happen soon, because there are more and more refugees arriving from the East. However, she has no news about how the Front is moving through Estonia. Very little is known about the war, because it is not written about in the newspapers or talked about on the radio.

My mother tells me that my father had to report for military service with the German army after we left. She had not mentioned this to me before. Now she hopes that he has not become part of the Eastern Front. We are increasingly worried about his safety.

As the September days go by, the air raids become more frequent. There are one or two or three air raids a day now. Our interrupted sleep makes us want to sleep during the day, or whenever we can. When raids occur during school time, we are often sent home. I begin to welcome these air raids, because I get out of school, and my new friends seem to feel as I do.

Often, we are told to run to a public air raid shelter nearby. This shelter has an opening on the side of a small hill. It is really a long cave with room for at least one hundred people. The walls and ceiling are made of large rocks and cement. The students, teachers, and townspeople sit on the stone benches along the sides and listen for the bombs. No one talks. Sometimes, when the sirens sound to announce that the danger is over, we are instructed to return to school. But recently, we are often told to go home and return to school the following day. I am glad to go home. Occasionally, I still go walking with my friends—or take a nap.

My mother tells me, during this time, that the large tin container of lard and pieces of bacon and onion which we have carried with us from Tuule Farm, is almost empty. We will have to totally rely on the weekly rations, which have been reduced. We no longer have meat with our meals because of the rationing.

The Müller's grandmother often meets us in the hallway leading to our room, with her apron folded up and containing some dried peas. My mother cooks pea soup everyday. It has become, along with bread, our main meal. I like it, because it is thick and it fills my stomach.

But there now are periods during the day when I feel hungry, and the hunger remains even when I go to bed at night, and actually, becomes worse when we are awakened by air raid sirens, and we have to go into the basement. We return to bed wanting food. We are all hungry. But we don't talk about it. Even at school. The farmers have the crops they raised, but the refugees and the townspeople must rely on the government rations.

Some evenings, after I complete my school assignments, I leave our room and walk down the street. The village is in total darkness. My friends in school have told me that this is because during the clear nights, when the bombers fly overhead, they will not be able to find targets to bomb if they cannot see lights from the house windows down below. At the farm, I notice that my mother hangs the grey Estonian blanket, from my grandmother, over our window at dusk and takes it down during the day.

My mother is very quiet. No word has been received about my father, and I can tell she is getting worried. She does not criticize me for anything. When I leave our room and see my friends, she never asks me where I have been. Also, she does not ask me about school or whether I have completed my assignments. She leaves me alone.

One particular school day, when the sirens go on, and we are sent home and told not to come back, I arrive at the Müller Farm earlier than usual. My mother tells me that as soon as the air raid danger is over, she wants the three of us to walk to the forest, a short distance behind the farm, and look for berries.

We wait, and then we walk quickly. As we reach the trees, we see red, hard berries on the bushes beneath them. She tells us that these are wild roses, and she can cook the berries and the end result will be a jam that we can spread on a piece of bread. We pick berries until darkness begins to arrive. My sister tries to help, but soon begins to cry because the thorns of the rose bushes are hurting her hands.

We return to our room, and my mother, after washing the berries, boils them. After awhile, the berries are reduced to a thick sauce, and she hands us pieces of bread covered with the thick pink sauce. As I begin to eat my piece of bread, I taste a sweet flavor, and I like it very much. My mother tells me that we will be eating mostly bread from here on, because the weekly rations only take care of our food for a couple of days, and we will have to eat this newly discovered berry paste as our food. She adds that she expects me to go on my own and pick these berries off the wild rose bushes. I am glad I can be of help with our food.

We are approaching the end of September, and we have not heard from our father. A group of refugees arrives one day, and my mother talks to several people who arrive on a truck. She describes my father to them, hoping that maybe some of them have seen him on their way across the Baltic. But no one has. A man in the group tells us that since this is already the latter part of September, he thinks the Eastern Front will sweep across the Baltic countries by October, and he adds, Estonia will probably be occupied by the Russian army even before then. I can see that my mother is even more worried, as we leave the group and return to the Müller Farm. I am worried, but I say nothing.

Except for the constant air raids, which interrupt our school days, I am getting bored. One day, my mother hands me a metal pail we use for getting milk from a store or a farmer. It holds about two liters, and she asks me to go to the Gasthaus and bring home some beer. Food is rationed. Beer is not.

She hands me some money and a note written to the tavern owner. I gladly walk to the Gasthaus and hand the container and the note to the man behind the counter. He glances at the note, then walks to a high faucet and slowly fills the container. After he pushes the cover on the pail, I hand him the money. He counts the coins and paper money and returns some of it to me, along with the small pail. He tells me that I should hurry home and that I should not open the pail. I thank him and quickly leave the Gasthaus.

Once out of sight of the tavern, I step into a doorway which is concealed from view. I look around and carefully take off the cover and place it on the ground. Then holding the sides of the pail with both hands, I raise it to my mouth—and slowly drink some of the bitter liquid. I repeat this about three times, carefully replace the cover, and slowly walk to the Müller Farm.

I deliver the pail to my mother, and she takes out two glasses, fills one, and pours a small amount into another glass. She hands me the small glass, and I thank her. I am relieved that she has not noticed that I already drank some of the beer.

I sit on my bed, and take small sips. My mother is doing the same, and again, I somehow feel that I am no longer a child. The bitter liquid fills my stomach, and I feel no hunger for food.

I tell my mother that I will rest, then I lie down on my bed and try to read a schoolbook. But I quickly fall asleep. I'm awakened by air raid sirens. The room is dark, and my mother is sleeping. I shake her by her shoulder and do the same to my sister, who is fast asleep beside her. Neither shows signs of waking, and the sirens sound again. The air raid danger has passed.

I fumble around the room looking for the pail of beer. I finally find it, but the cover is gone. I shake the pail and hear some liquid making a sound inside. I raise the pail to my lips and slowly drink the small amount of bitter liquid. I return the pail to where I found it. I walk close to my mother, and she, as well as my sister, is still asleep. I return to my bed, and promptly fall asleep.

The walk to the Gasthaus becomes a daily task for me. My mother no longer sends a note. When I walk in, the man at the Gasthaus immediately takes the metal container and fills it, counts the money that I place on the counter, and returns the rest. On the way back to the Müller Farm, I duck into the same doorway and drink some of the beer, then slowly walk the rest of the way.

When I am back in our room, my mother pours me half a glass, and I sip it, slowly allowing the bitter liquid to drain down my throat. It immediately fills my stomach, and I feel no hunger.

Chapter 32.

A MAN COMES TO GRAITSCHEN

One day, when I return from school and am about to enter our room, I hear a man's voice coming from the inside. I press one side of my head against the door to hear better, and I suddenly think the man inside could be my father. I walk in and see him sitting on a chair, holding my sister on his lap. As soon as he sees me, he gets up, puts my sister down, and walks up to me with his hand extended. We shake hands, and he says my mother has told him that I have been very helpful since we left Estonia, nearly two months ago. He adds that he is glad I am in school again.

I remain silent about my dislike for school and how I welcome the air raids that so often disrupt it. I also think to myself, that with my father's arrival, I will no longer be looked at as somehow being the leader of the family. Although I am glad to see my father, I almost wish that he would not have arrived so soon.

He is wearing several layers of clothing, and has four inflated bicycle tubes around his waist and chest. He says he took this bicycle tube precaution because, if his ship were sunk by the Russian navy or air force, he would have a chance of floating. If the sinking happened near shore, he would then be able to reach land.

In answer to our many questions, he says that he and others in the Estonian unit were given permission to either stay, or leave. He made up his mind to leave because he could see there was no hope of holding back the advancing Russians. He decided to go to Tallinn and try to escape to Germany by ship.

My father briefly describes his trip. He left Tallinn about ten days ago. He and a man pushing a cart loaded with my father's suitcases, started together from Piirita. My father walked faster, and was able to take a shortcut, and reach the harbor safely because he was only carrying his large briefcase, with money and some Russian czarist gold coins. The Russian army arrived before the man with the cart was able to reach the harbor, and the area was sealed off by the Russian soldiers. My father never saw this man, or the cart, again.

He goes on to say that he was about to board a certain ship, when he noticed that this ship was listing heavily to one side. He then decided to board another ship, and when he arrived in Danzig, he learned that the listing ship had been sunk by Russian torpedoes, resulting in the loss of several thousand refugees.

Upon his arrival in Danzig, he boarded a train which took him to my mother's distant relative's home, where he learned of our new location. He next continued by train to Jena, and then walked to Graitschen, because there was no other transportation.

After hearing his story, filled with close calls, I am glad that he is again with us. However, I now begin thinking of ways to avoid discussing my school assignments—especially mathematics, my most hated subject. But one that I know he feels is very important for when I become a banker.

That evening we all walk to the Gasthaus. It is getting dark, and the large windows are dark, covered with shades. As we enter, we find the large room nearly full of people who are speaking loudly and laughing happily.

We find a table, and a woman with a white apron speaks to my parents, who order beer and ham sandwiches. My father digs one of his hands deep into a pocket of his coat and places a pile of paper money on the table. The woman with the white apron picks it up and takes it to the man behind the bar. The man looks in our direction and waves his hand. I notice that the pile of paper money needed for food seems to get larger every day.

Shortly, the woman returns carrying a tray filled with foaming glasses of beer. Next to the large glasses is a smaller glass half-full of beer. She places it in front of me. I look at my father, who nods his head, and then I know it is all right for me to drink the beer.

After finishing our meal, which is the first full meal we have eaten in a long time, we all leave the Gasthaus and head down the dark street to the Müller Farm. As we enter the yard, the air raid sirens start blowing their familiar sound, and rather than go to our room, we enter the basement, where I quickly find my usual place on a pile of potatoes. After the sirens sound again, we return to our room, and without removing my outer clothing, I lie down on my bed and fall asleep.

The days go by quickly. The arrival of my father has brought some changes in my life, however. He is much more interested, than is my mother, in whether I complete my school assignments, and when I come home from school he insists that I do my mathematics lessons. This makes my life a little more difficult. But he continues to insist that I do well, because he still wants me to become a banker when I grow up. He becomes angry when I do poorly on this homework and often raises his arms above his head, saying loudly, "How can you do poorly in mathematics?"

So whenever I return from school, my life is no longer the same. The other very definite change in my life, is the fact that my mother no longer looks at me as an adult. She again sees me as a child of ten years old. She tells me that when the villagers learned that my father is a banker, they suddenly began to call her Frau Taagen. I think she is trying to convince me to work harder on my homework, so I can be a banker, too.

Naturally, I try to stay away from home as much as possible. My mother always asks me what I am doing when I am away from the Müller Farm, and I always manage to bring home pockets filled with rose berries, which I quickly gather as an excuse for being away. But the truth is, I usually spend these times away visiting with my friends from school.

One Saturday, when I am home, Herr Müller asks my parents to accompany him to his fields outside the village. I ask him if I can also go along, and he tells me that I can. He takes all of us, along with his sons, on a wagon that he pulls with a tractor. We go up a hill and arrive in a field of grapes. We are given hoes with long handles and asked to dig up the weeds. As we dig, it is expected that we can eat some grapes. We work for several hours, after which time he removes a large basket from the wagon and tells us to eat. The basket holds slices of rye bread and a dish filled with slices of sausage.

I quickly grab two large slices of bread and place several slices of sausage between them. I sit on the ground, take one large bite after another, and the hunger I have felt for what seems forever, begins to disappear. After I have finished my sandwich, Herr Müller tells me to eat a slice of a cake that's filled with pieces of dark blue plums. We have not seen cake since our first night with the Müllers. It tastes wonderful.

After we work until well into the afternoon, Herr Müller tells us we can now return to his farm in the village. After this, I always look forward to working, because I know that there will always be food when I work for Herr Müller. I wish he needed us every day. But he does not.

1. Author arriving in homeland, Tallinn, Estonia, September 9, 1999.

2. Author arriving in homeland, Tallinn, Estonia, Sept. 9, 1999, with sister and others.

3. Tallinn Harbor with relatives, September 9, 1999.

4. Cemetery visit.

5. Author reunited with cousin, Hille Tagen Olvet, his closest living relative in Estonia.

6. Bank building, Tallinn Street, Viljandi.

7. Gateway to castle built by Teutonic Knights, 1200s, Viljandi.

8. Barn at Tuule (Wind) Farm.

9. Old Walled City, Tallinn.

10. Old Town Square, Tallinn.

11. Old Town Square, Tallinn. Author and Hiie Olvet Laugesaar.

12. Paternal grandparents with sons, Alfred and Johannes. Johannes is wearing his Tartu University cap.

13. Fraternity gathering, winter, 1936, Viljandi. Johannes is kissing woman in back row. Ludmilla is in front row, third from right.

14. Author's parents with maternal grandfather. Assumed to be before 1934. Couple on left is unidentified.

15. Author's baptism, 1934.

16. Author with mother, 1934.

17. Seaside resort, Pärnu, 1935. Author on mother's lap.
Author's father on right.

18. Author's home and family, May, 1939, Viljandi.

19. Author and sister, Linda, behind their home in field of daisies.

20. Author and sister, Linda, approximately 1943.

21. Tuule Farm, with surveyors, family, and friends, approximately 1940.

22. Jaanipäev (Saint John's Day), longest day of year. Family at Tuule Farm, June, 1942.

23. Moltkefels, ship on which author, mother, and sister sailed from Tallinn to Germany in August, 1944.

24. Entrance to second DP Camp 563, Wiesbaden, Germany.

25. Wiesbaden, DP camp building.

26. Author and Boy Scout friends, Wiesbaden, 1946 (see cover illustration). Bombed building in background.

27. YMCA summer camp near Geislingen.

28. Author with other campers, 1948.

29. Author, Geislingen an Steige, 1949, in front of home where the family lived. Shortly before leaving for America.

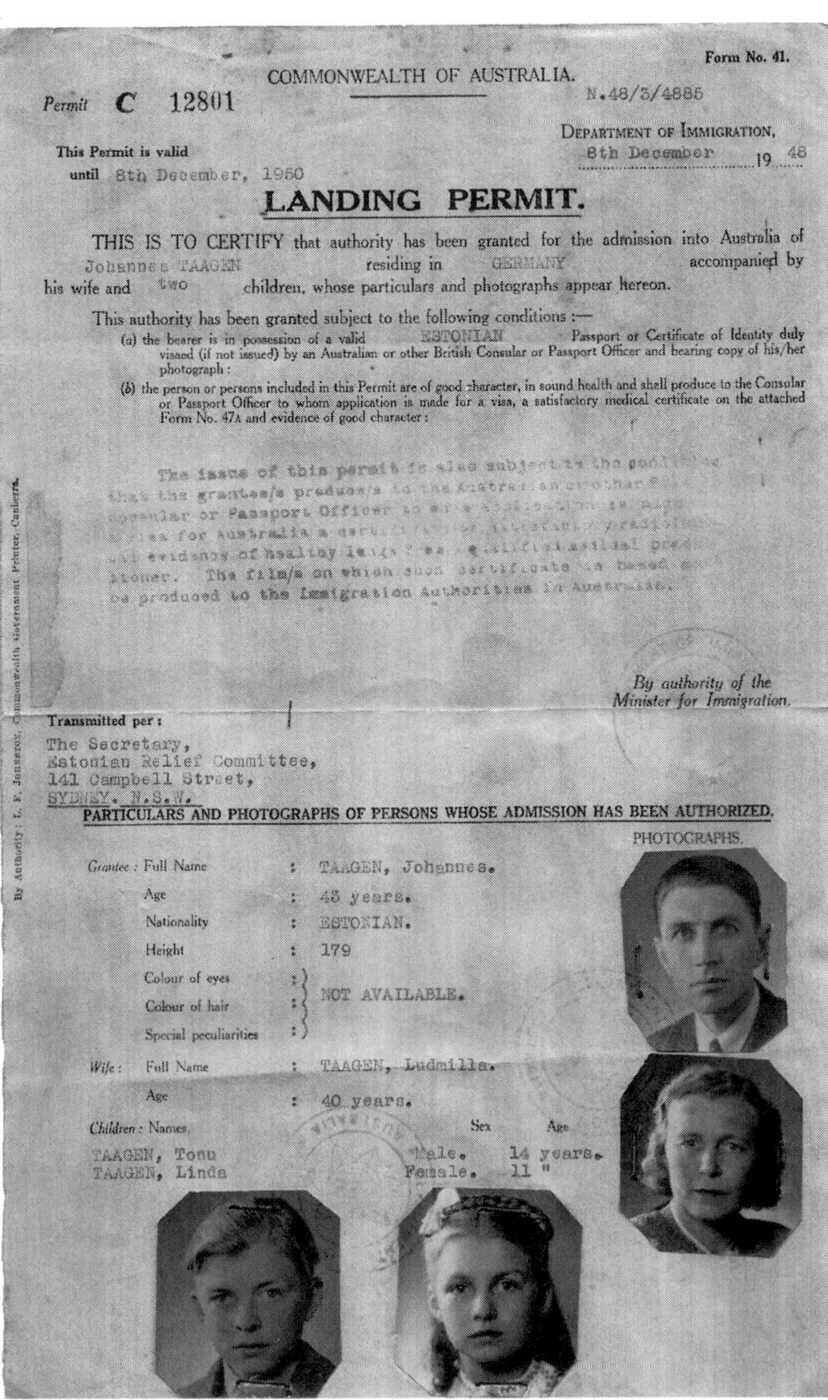

Form No. 41.

COMMONWEALTH OF AUSTRALIA.

Permit **C** 12801

N.48/3/4885

DEPARTMENT OF IMMIGRATION,
8th December 19 48

This Permit is valid until 8th December, 1950

LANDING PERMIT.

THIS IS TO CERTIFY that authority has been granted for the admission into Australia of Johannes TAAGEN residing in GERMANY accompanied by his wife and two children, whose particulars and photographs appear hereon.

This authority has been granted subject to the following conditions :—

(*a*) the bearer is in possession of a valid ESTONIAN Passport or Certificate of Identity duly visaed (if not issued) by an Australian or other British Consular or Passport Officer and bearing copy of his/her photograph :

(*b*) the person or persons included in this Permit are of good character, in sound health and shall produce to the Consular or Passport Officer to whom application is made for a visa, a satisfactory medical certificate on the attached Form No. 47A and evidence of good character :

The issue of this permit is also subject [illegible] that the grantee/s produce/s [illegible] Consular or Passport Officer [illegible] for Australia a [illegible] evidence of healthy lungs [illegible] tioner. The film/s on which such [illegible] be produced to the Immigration Authorities [illegible]

By authority of the Minister for Immigration.

Transmitted per :

The Secretary,
Estonian Relief Committee,
141 Campbell Street,
SYDNEY. N.S.W.

PARTICULARS AND PHOTOGRAPHS OF PERSONS WHOSE ADMISSION HAS BEEN AUTHORIZED.

PHOTOGRAPHS.

Grantee : Full Name : TAAGEN, Johannes.
Age : 43 years.
Nationality : ESTONIAN.
Height : 179
Colour of eyes / Colour of hair / Special peculiarities : NOT AVAILABLE.

Wife : Full Name : TAAGEN, Ludmilla.
Age : 40 years.

Children : Names	Sex	Age
TAAGEN, Toom	Male.	14 years.
TAAGEN, Linda	Female.	11 "

By Authority : L. F. Johnston, Commonwealth Government Printer, Canberra.

30. Landing Permit for Australia.

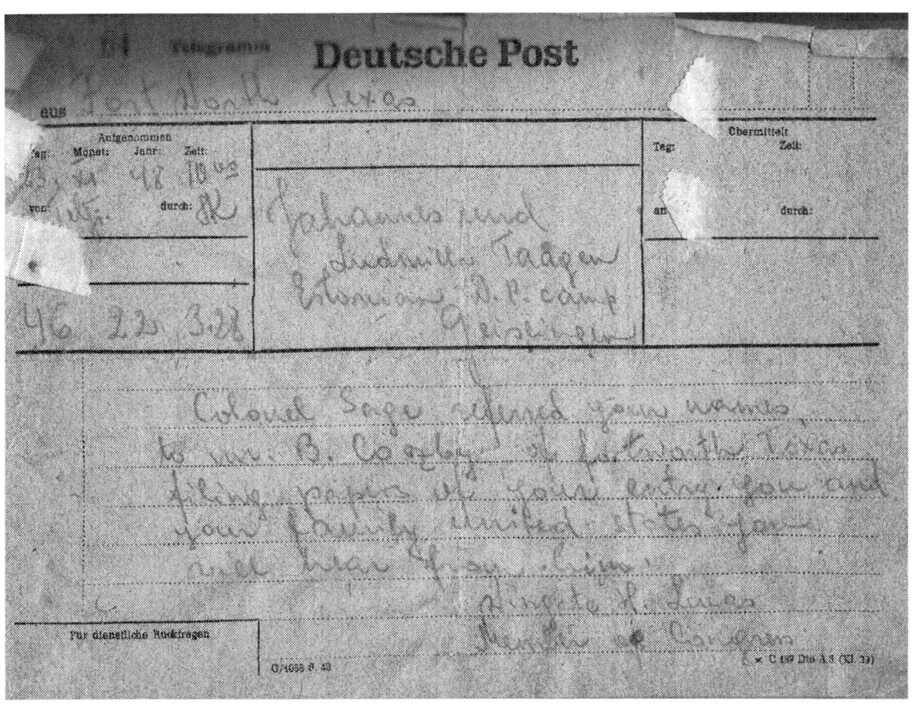

Telegramm **Deutsche Post**

aus Fort Worth Texas

Aufgenommen
Tag: Monat: Jahr: Zeit:
von: durch:

Übermittelt
Tag: Zeit:
an durch:

Colonel Sage

Für dienstliche Rückfragen

31. Telegram from Wingate Lucas, Texas congressman.

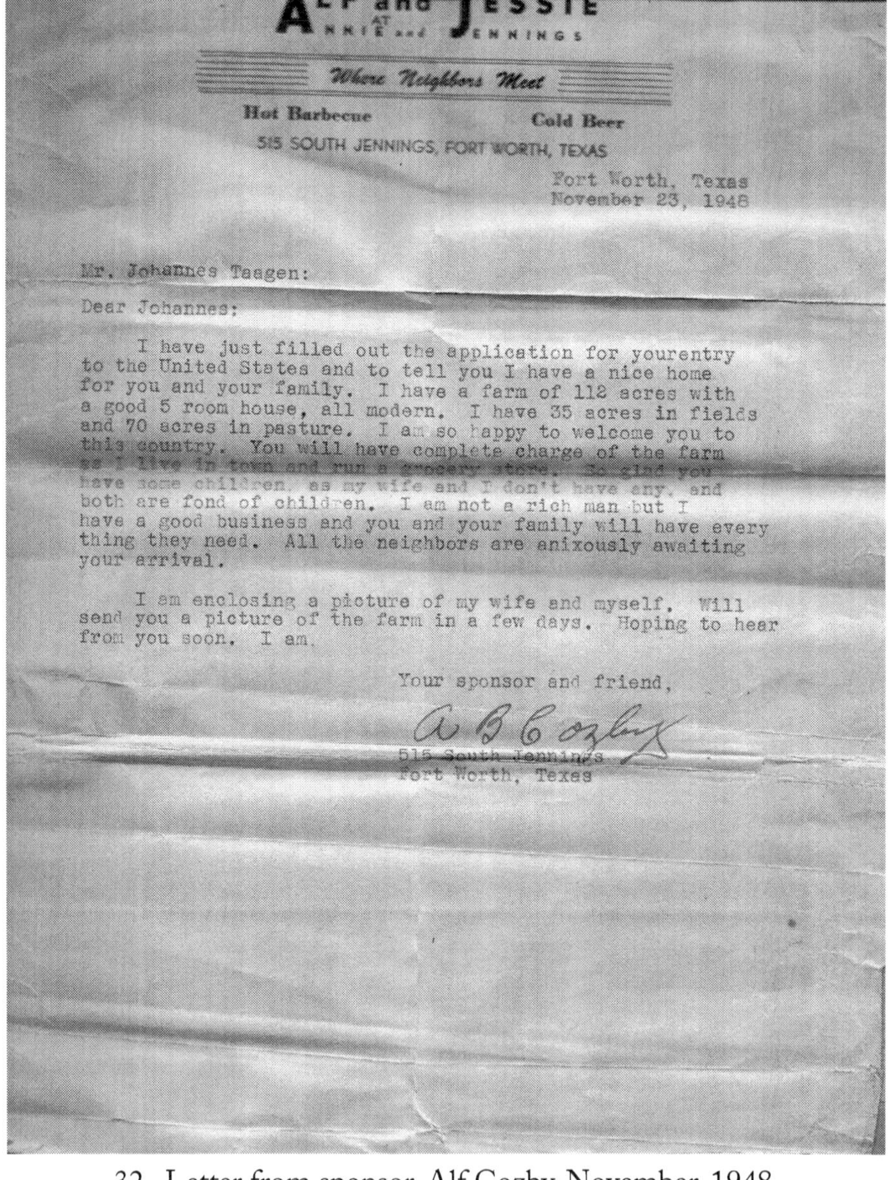

ALF and JESSIE
AT
ANNIE and JENNINGS

Where Neighbors Meet

Hot Barbecue **Cold Beer**

515 SOUTH JENNINGS, FORT WORTH, TEXAS

Fort Worth, Texas
November 23, 1948

Mr. Johannes Taagen:

Dear Johannes:

I have just filled out the application for yourentry to the United States and to tell you I have a nice home for you and your family. I have a farm of 112 acres with a good 5 room house, all modern. I have 35 acres in fields and 70 acres in pasture. I am so happy to welcome you to this country. You will have complete charge of the farm as I live in town and run a grocery store. So glad you have some children, as my wife and I don't have any, and both are fond of children. I am not a rich man but I have a good business and you and your family will have every thing they need. All the neighbors are anixously awaiting your arrival.

I am enclosing a picture of my wife and myself. Will send you a picture of the farm in a few days. Hoping to hear from you soon. I am,

Your sponsor and friend,

A B Cozby

515 South Jennings
Fort Worth, Texas

32. Letter from sponsor, Alf Cozby, November, 1948.

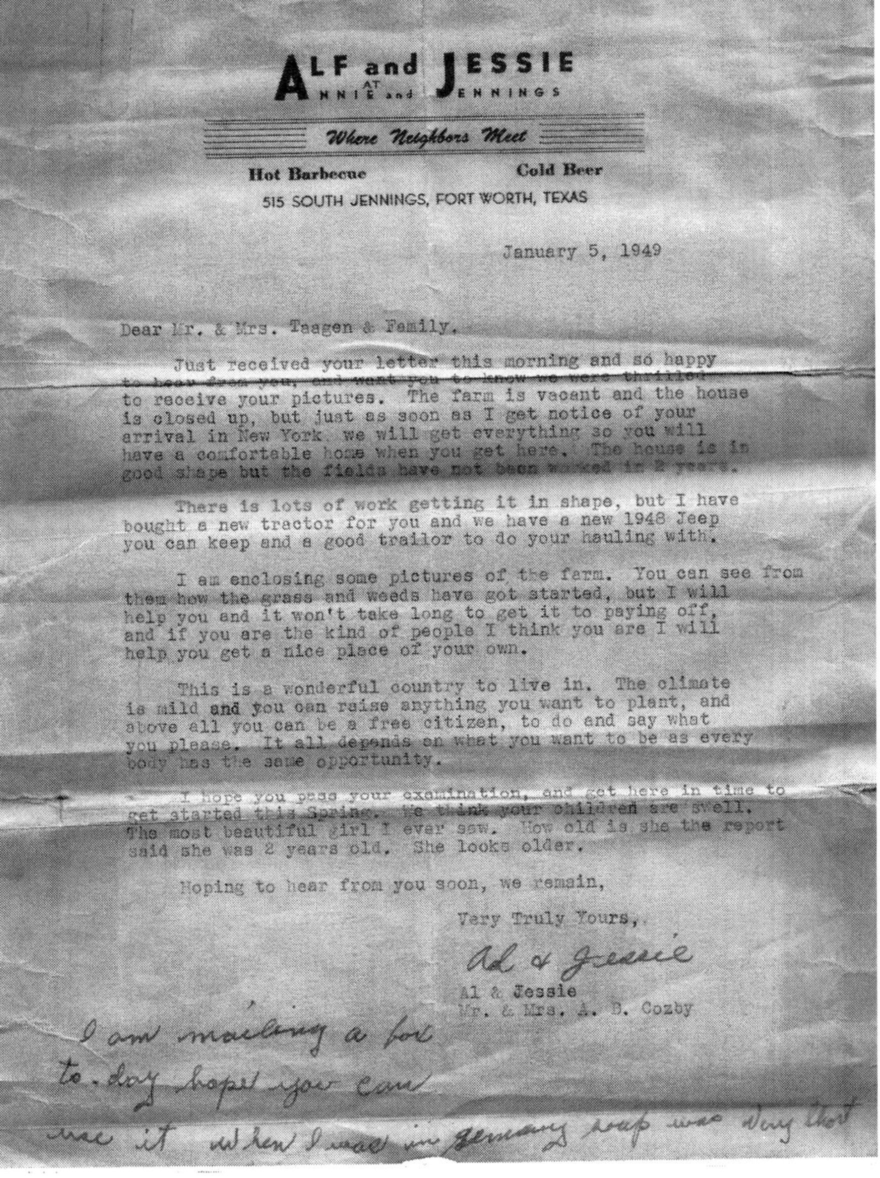

ALF and JESSIE
AT ANNIE and JENNINGS

Where Neighbors Meet

Hot Barbecue **Cold Beer**

515 SOUTH JENNINGS, FORT WORTH, TEXAS

January 5, 1949

Dear Mr. & Mrs. Taagen & Family.

Just received your letter this morning and so happy to hear from you, and want you to know we were thrilled to receive your pictures. The farm is vacant and the house is closed up, but just as soon as I get notice of your arrival in New York, we will get everything so you will have a comfortable home when you get here. The house is in good shape but the fields have not been worked in 2 years.

There is lots of work getting it in shape, but I have bought a new tractor for you and we have a new 1948 Jeep you can keep and a good trailor to do your hauling with.

I am enclosing some pictures of the farm. You can see from them how the grass and weeds have got started, but I will help you and it won't take long to get it to paying off, and if you are the kind of people I think you are I will help you get a nice place of your own.

This is a wonderful country to live in. The climate is mild and you can raise anything you want to plant, and above all you can be a free citizen, to do and say what you please. It all depends on what you want to be as every body has the same opportunity.

I hope you pass your examination, and get here in time to get started this Spring. We think your children are swell. The most beautiful girl I ever saw. How old is she the report said she was 2 years old. She looks older.

Hoping to hear from you soon, we remain,

Very Truly Yours,

Al & Jessie

Al & Jessie
Mr. & Mrs. A. B. Cozby

I am mailing a box to-day hope you can use it When I was in Germany soap was very short

33. Letter from Alf and Jessie Cozby, January, 1949.

34. Alfred and Jessie Cozby.

35. Author and other Estonian refugees leaving Geislingen by truck, February 7, 1949.

36. Author, back row between mother and father, and other Estonian passengers on the Marine Tiger.

37. Author on board Marine Tiger wearing fur cap.

38. Arrival in New York, February 27, 1949. Family with Mr. Cozby in front of unnamed hotel.

39. Arrival in Texas, March 2, 1949.

40. Housewarming, Springtown, Texas.

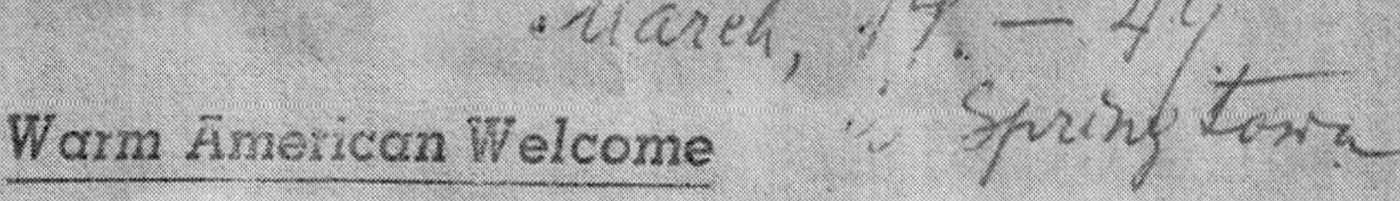

March 14 — 49
Springtown

Warm American Welcome

Neighbors Greet Refugee Estonian Family in Their New Farm Home

BY JANICE CONLEY.
Star-Telegram Staff Writer.

SPRINGTOWN, March 14.—Residents of Parker County Monday extended a warm American welcome to a refugee Estonian family at their new farm home near here.

Neighbors from far and wide, business men and their families from Springtown and Weatherford, and county agricultural officials employed the grand old custom of house warming to make their neighbors from across the ocean feel at home in the community.

The honored guests, Mr. and Mrs. John Taagen, who arrived in the United States March 2 with their two children, were amazed at first when neighbors trotted in bearing gifts from the wealth of their land. There were canned fruits and vegetables, personal gifts for their home, fresh foods, and even five laying hens.

Before the day was over, Mrs. Taagen gathered in the first harvest—a shiny white egg.

The Taagens soon got into the spirit of the thing and began to show off their new home—a five-room frame house equipped with butane gas and electricity, refrigerator, and even a washing machine. For his work in the fields on the 112-acre farm, Taagen has a new tractor and other equipment.

Mr. and Mrs. A. B. Cozby of Fort Worth, who "adopted" the family and arranged to bring them here from a displaced persons camp in Germany, were hosts at a barbecue for all of the guests. Against a background of hillbilly music from a loudspeaker system, the Taagens chatted in halting English and became acquainted with their new neighbors.

Mrs. Taagen makes herself learn 10 new English words each day from an Estonian-English dictionary which they bought before coming to the United States. Taagen speaks English fairly easily, but their son, Tony, is the best in the family and corrects both his parents and his young sister, Linda.

Cozby, who owns a grocery business in Fort Worth, turned over his farm to the Taagens for their new home. He and Taagen conferred at length Monday with County Agent J. O. Woodman of Parker County and Harvey C. White, Soil Conservation Service worker from Weatherford, about crops for the land. Taagen already has begun plowing his fields, and expects to put in truck produce. Later, Cozby may buy a dairy herd for the farm.

—Star-Telegram Staff Photo.

MRS. JOHN TAAGEN, right, shows off the first egg to Mrs. A. B. Cozby.

41. Housewarming newspaper article and photo of mother and sponsor, Jessie Cozby.

42. Author driving tractor, summer, 1949.

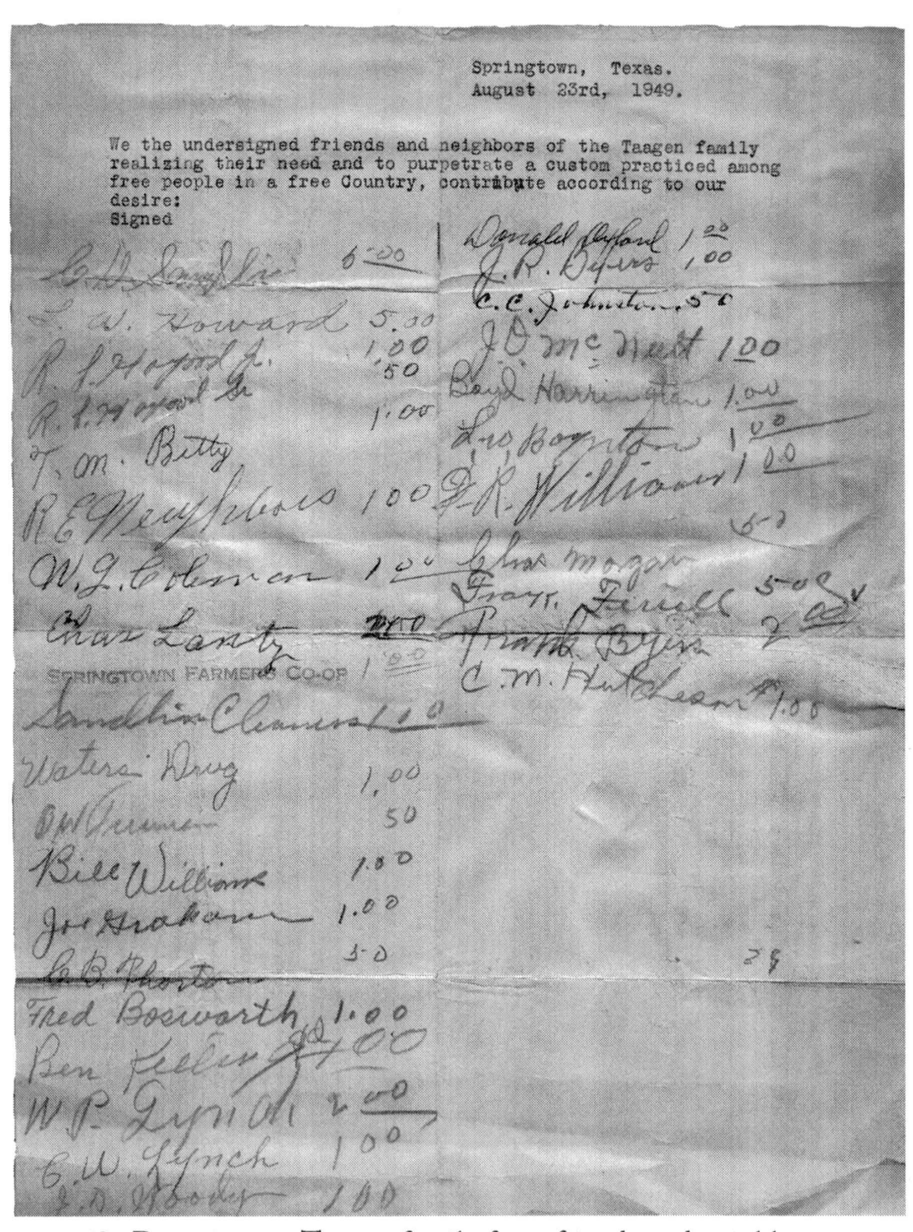

Springtown, Texas.
August 23rd, 1949.

We the undersigned friends and neighbors of the Taagen family realizing their need and to purpetrate a custom practiced among free people in a free Country, contribute according to our desire:
Signed

SPRINGTOWN FARMERS CO-OP

43. Donations to Taagen family from friends and neighbors.

D. P. Attends High School Here

44. Author, high school, West Bend, Wisconsin.

Chapter 33.

THE BOMBER, BEEHIVE, MORE BOMBS, AND BEER

One morning, when I arrive at school, there is a rumor that an American bomber was shot down during the night, and it crashed somewhere in the woods between Graitschen and Jena.

During the break at lunchtime, my two friends ask me if I would like to accompany them to where the plane is. They seem to have an idea where it happened, and they think it's about an hour's walk.

After school we set out on our way. I stop to tell my parents that I will not be home at the usual time because one of my friends needs help on their farm. I know that if I tell the truth, I will not be allowed to go, because I am required to do my mathematics lesson after school.

My parents give their approval, and we start walking through fields and wooded areas. After about an hour's walk, we see a pile of dark metal in the distance. And as we get closer, now running, we realize that it is an airplane that is partially burned.

At the site of the crash, we see that there is very little left. We see no dead bodies, and think the crew parachuted out before the crash. As we walk through what is left of the plane, one of my friends says there might be some chocolate buried in the ashes. After about a half hour of digging, we find nothing, except some machine gun shells that have exploded in the fire. We divide the few shells that we find, place them in our pockets, and resume the tiring walk back to Graitschen. How disappointing. We had expected to find unexploded shells, or chocolate.

When we arrive, we split up, and each of us returns home. When I get back, I am greeted by my father, who is angry and insists that I do my mathematics lesson—immediately. My father tells me that they are going to the Gasthaus, but I must stay behind and finish my lessons. I nod. And as soon as they leave, I empty my pockets of the exploded machine gun shells and hide them under my mattress. Then I begin the boring math lessons.

When my parents return from the Gasthaus, I pretend that my lessons are finished. They have brought back the metal container full of beer. I ask if I can have some, and my mother pours me a half glass. I take the glass outside, sit in the yard on a low brick wall, and sip the beer slowly. Again it makes me feel good, and I forget the boring math lessons.

Another day, Herr Müller asks my father if he is able to build him a bee hive. My father knows what to do, because his uncle had been a carpenter and had taught him when my father was growing up. Herr Müller tells my father that tomorrow morning, he will have the wood and tools ready.

My father seems to enjoy what he is doing. After several days, the wood hive, which looks like a little house, is finished, and when Herr Müller looks at it he nods his head in approval. He tells my father to wait while he goes into the house. He returns shortly, carrying a rifle.

Some pigeons are sitting on the top of the house. Herr Müller takes aim—and fires. Immediately, a pigeon drops over and rolls off the roof, hitting the ground. The group of pigeons that had been sitting on the roof soon return. Apparently, they are not aware that one of them has been shot. Herr Müller again raises his rifle, takes aim, and fires. Another pigeon drops over and rolls off the roof. Herr Müller walks over to the dead pigeons, picks them off the ground, walks over to my father, and hands them to him as payment for the perfect beehive. My father is thankful. Herr Müller has been kind enough to provide us with housing, and that is all we expect.

My father tells me we will be eating the pigeons tonight.

My mother decides to make the pigeons into soup. After my father has removed their feathers and insides, and they have boiled for awhile, my mother removes the bones and cuts the pigeons into small pieces. She puts the pieces back into the hot water and adds some more water and many peeled potatoes. She tells me we will have soup for three days, and it will taste like chicken, a flavor we have not experienced since the Tuule Farm.

While the soup is cooking, she hands me the tin container and tells me to go to the Gasthaus and get beer. She hands me a handful of crumpled paper money and tells me to hurry. As I enter the Gasthaus, the man behind the bar waves his hand in my direction and motions for me to come forward. He seems to know what I want, and takes the metal container from me. He fills it, then pours me a half glass of beer. I stand next to the raised counter and slowly begin to drink, as the man behind the bar counts money from the handful of paper money and coins. He hands me back some money, and I stuff it into my pocket.

I sip the beer, and as I look around, I see no others my age in the Gasthaus. Once again, I feel like an adult and not a child. After finishing my beer, I thank the man behind the counter, pick up the container of beer, and leave the Gasthaus. I think it would be wonderful if I could have stayed in the Gasthaus a little longer, because it is such a friendly place, and when I am there I feel happy and no longer think of the war that has been going on for what seems to me like a very long time with no end in sight. Neither does there seem to be an end in sight for school.

As I walk back to the Müller Farm, I walk past the dark doorway where I have stopped before. I enter the doorway quickly, pry open the cover to the metal container, raise the container with both hands, and take a large swallow. After carefully putting on the metal cover, I continue to the Müller Farm.

When I enter our room, my mother asks me why it took me so long, and I tell her that I came across some students from my class and that

I found out more about a lesson that I had not completed. She seems satisfied with my answer and fills two large glasses with beer for herself and my father. She also pours a half-full glass and hands it to me.

I sit on my bed, with the glass, and start to sip it slowly. My parents are seated at the table with my sister, who seems to be upset because I was given some beer, while she was not. My mother gets a small piece of bread and covers it with some jam made out of the cooked rose berries, and this seems to please her.

After my parents finish their glasses of beer, we all sit at the table and eat the soup made from the pigeons. It is very good and filling, and it does taste like chicken.

Then everyone lies down and falls asleep, only to be awakened by the nightly air raid sirens. We all descend into the basement to await the all-clear siren, after which, we can return to our beds. My sister has already fallen asleep in the basement, and my father carries her to our room. As soon as I lie down on my bed, I fall asleep.

Days, as they pass, become weeks. The only difference is that the air raids are becoming more frequent and more unpredictable. Sometimes, Herr Müller allows me to leave the basement before the second siren's sound. Herr Müller, wearing his helmet, and I, watch the sky over Jena, which is illuminated by search lights from the ground. Occasionally, we hear the sound of antiaircraft fire directed at the bombers overhead. Being able to watch the sky makes it much more exciting. It is much better than sitting on a pile of potatoes in the basement as we wait for a siren indicating that a raid has passed.

Chapter 34.

SEARCHING FOR VALDO

When I return home from school one day, my parents tell me that we are going to walk to a neighboring town, because a train filled with wounded soldiers from the Eastern Front has stopped there.

Valdo must have received our new address from the distant relative near Berlin, because we have received occasional letters from him indicating that he is somewhere on the Eastern Front. We are so relieved when we receive these letters.

As we reach the train station, we see many rail cars displaying a large red cross outlined in white. My father explains to me that under certain rules of war, a train marked with these symbols cannot be attacked by airplanes, because it is carrying soldiers who are no longer a part of the war.

As we approach the train, we see soldiers at the windows looking out, often their heads wrapped with bandages which show signs of dried, dark red blood. The train is surrounded by people, mostly women, moving along and trying to look inside, in hopes that their husband or son or brother or nephew may be on board—and still alive.

My father asks me to stay with my sister, as he and my mother begin to walk along the side of the train and try to look in. If there is a wounded soldier at an open window, my father asks him if he knows a Valdo Tagen. This question is always answered by the wounded soldier shaking his head.

Some of the women, as they walk along the platform, hold pictures of their family member to the window, in hopes that one of the wounded will recognize them. However, every time a picture is held up to the window, the men inside shake their heads.

After about an hour of looking for Valdo, or someone who might know him, my father decides that we should return to Graitschen, because it is getting dark. He picks up my sister, and we begin our walk back to Graitschen.

As I walk behind my parents, I think back to the heads wrapped in bloody bandages looking out of the open windows on the train, and I think of the war, and I wonder how long it will last, and I realize that, in my memory, I can only remember there being war.

When we arrive in Graitschen, my father tells us that we will eat supper at the Gasthaus. My father orders soup and beer. When the beer arrives, carried by a waitress, I notice a small glass filled to the half. She places that glass in front of me. This makes me feel good, because I know now that the man behind the bar knows me, and this again makes me feel as though I am an adult, or at least an adult ten-year-old.

I eat my soup, and when my bowl is empty, I take the beer and begin to drink it slowly. My mother looks at me and shakes her finger in my direction. But she does not say anything. I now feel that I have her approval to drink beer.

When we return to the Müller Farm, I go to bed—only to be awakened again by the sirens that mean another trip to the basement.

Chapter 35.

PLUMS, A NEW STUDENT, AND RUSSIAN PRISONERS

A few days later, while I am sitting outside, Herr Müller tells me that there is a plum tree behind the house, and I may shake the tree and have the plums that fall to the ground. I have seen this tree. I immediately go to it, pick out a low branch, and shake it. Many plums fall to the ground. I remove my jacket, place it on the ground, and start gathering the fallen fruit and putting it on the jacket. Then I fold the jacket so that I can easily carry the plums to our room.

But before taking them to our room, I decide to eat some of the plums, because I am hungry. Before I know it, I have eaten half of them. I then carry the rest to our room and hand them to my mother, explaining how I received the plums. My stomach feels very full, and I lie on my bed and begin to read a schoolbook—and shortly fall asleep.

I don't know how long I sleep, but I awaken with a bad stomachache. I lie on my side and move my knees closer to my chest, hoping that this will help the awful pain. But the pain remains. I begin to moan. I try to tell my mother what has happened. She seems to understand my problem, walks over to the tin container holding some beer, and pours it into a small glass, then adds a white powdery substance to the beer and stirs it with a spoon. She tells me that the powder is used for baking bread, and she tells me to drink the beer, which is now foaming. I empty the glass and, again, lie down. In a short while, the pain has disappeared. I thank my mother and promptly fall asleep. And sleep through our evening meal.

For the rest of the autumn, very little happens to change my life. There is a continual shortage of food, but my parents seem to have enough money for visits to the Gasthaus and for an occasional bowl of vegetable soup. Sometimes, in the village, we see other Estonian refugees who are also staying at farms in Graitschen or the nearby villages. My parents have not known them in Estonia, but because we are now all refugees, they quickly become friends.

One day, a new student arrives in school. He is brought by his mother. The teacher introduces the boy to the class as being from Westphalia. The teacher opens a large map, which is rolled up above the blackboard, and with a long stick points out the region where the boy came from. It is near Holland. The boy is well dressed and wears a suit that does not seem to fit in well with the clothing worn by the rest of the class.

A few days later, we are in the exercise yard behind the school, and some of us start to make fun of him because he is so differently dressed. He later complains to the teacher, and three of us are singled out and ordered to come to the front of the class. The teacher tells us that we will be punished for making fun of the new student.

He tells us to stand facing the class, and tells the first boy to bend over. He does. Then, the teacher hits him five times across his rear with the long wooden stick normally used to point out places on the blackboard.

This first boy yells out in pain, and the teacher tells him to return to his desk. As the teacher orders the second boy to bend over, the air raid sirens begin to howl. He tells the second boy about to receive the whipping, and me, that class is dismissed, but we will be punished when we return to school. We are both relieved for now, and promptly leave school.

When we return the following day, we expect to be punished. Nothing happens. The teacher apparently has forgotten about the punishment, which we had worried about all night. We are very relieved. As the days go on, the three of us include the boy from Westphalia in our small group of friends.

One day, when I'm standing near the street, I see a long column of men approaching. They are surrounded by German soldiers. As they get closer, I see this column of men walking and staggering. They are Russian prisoners, I am told by a woman standing near me. They are dressed in shabby, dark uniforms. Some wear hats with flaps covering their ears and concealing parts of their faces.

As the first column passes, I notice some prisoners wearing uniforms that seem clean, and the men wearing them are walking straight, without a stagger. The woman next to me tells me that these are English soldiers and comments that they look much better than the Russians. As the column passes us, it also passes a wagon being pulled by an ox, and loaded with white sugar beets. The farmer is walking next to it. Some beets fall from the wagon, and several Russians at the end of their line drop to their knees and try to pick up the beets, in hopes of being able to eat them on the spot.

But as they stagger, while trying to get a footing, they drop the beets to the road. The English soldiers, immediately behind them, pick up the fallen beets, and as they pass the wagon, place the beets back on it.

The woman next to me remarks, "See those Russians stealing, but the British are more cultured and return the stolen goods." I wonder, to myself, if the English soldiers have been treated better, and are not starving.

Chapter 36.

LATE 1944, CHRISTMAS, EARLY 1945, TELEGRAM ABOUT VALDO

My daily life has become very uneventful. School is not a problem, except for math, and the air raids have not changed in their daily and nightly habits. I make frequent visits into the woods surrounding the village with my friends, where we gather rose berries for my mother, who cooks them into jam.

Occasionally, we walk along the road leading into the village, but my friends warn me that if there are army trucks going down the road, they can attract aircraft, and if they attack the army trucks, we can easily get killed. They tell me of attacks happening west of here, where cities are connected by major roads. In any event, this has not prevented us from walking along the road, and sometimes even to Bürgel, which we still visit often.

I find occasional chances to get beer at the Gasthaus for my parents, and the man behind the counter knows me and always rewards me with a small glass of beer not quite filled to the top. These visits make me feel good, because sometimes other patrons ask me questions about my fleeing from Estonia, and this makes me feel like an adult, and not a child—the rank my parents give to me, especially, since my father arrived from the East. Also, because some say I am tall for my age, I like to think they believe I am older than I am.

Time is passing, and we are getting close to Christmas, but the feeling of looking forward to that time is not there. It seems war is replacing that great feeling, when I used to look forward to presents, and special foods, and my grandfather's delivery of our Christmas tree. These are no longer part of my life.

As Christmas approaches, my father and mother seem to have increased their walks to the Gasthaus. Although I am often told that I can stay in our room with my sister while they are gone, I prefer to go along, if for no other reason than the man behind the counter, who always pours me a half glass of beer. And as I sip my beer slowly, it still makes me feel good, and it makes the hunger disappear. Besides that, my parents always seem to be in a better mood, and the serious conversation is often replaced by laughter.

When the morning of Christmas Eve arrives, the Müller's grandmother comes to our room, carrying a plate filled with a variety of sliced sausages and a loaf of freshly baked rye bread. My mother gratefully thanks the old woman, and they exchange Christmas greetings.

That afternoon, we all go to the Gasthaus which is filled with people, and after my parents have finished several glasses of beer, and I have had several half glasses of beer, we leave. Before walking out, my father approaches a woman who serves people at tables, and they exchange some words. The woman then goes into an adjoining room and returns with two bottles. My father hands her a stack of paper money, which she places in her apron pocket, and we leave.

When we are outside, my father tells me that the woman was kind to sell us some wine. He also tells us she has a son on the Eastern Front, but has not heard from him for several weeks. It seems the Eastern Front turns strangers into persons who are united. Over the past few months, this feeling has become more and more evident to me, as time goes on, and the Front itself is getting closer and closer.

Back in our room my mother prepares sandwiches of the sausage slices from the Müllers. We all eat, and once again my stomach is full, and I feel no hunger. My father opens a bottle of wine, and the adults fill their glasses.

My mother looks at me, then picks up a glass and pours in some wine, barely covering the bottom of the glass. As she is about to hand it to me, she turns to the bottle, and pours some more wine into the glass, and then hands it to me saying, "Merry Christmas."

My parents soon begin to talk about the relatives that stayed behind—wondering what they are doing at this time, wondering if they are even alive. The conversation then turns to Valdo, my cousin, who is somewhere on the Eastern Front. My mother picks up my sister, places her on her lap, and sits down at the table. As I look at her, I see that she is crying, and my sister, looking into her eyes, also begins to cry. My father walks over to her, and motions to me to come over, and before long everyone in the room is crying.

I think of earlier Christmases, and I remember happy people laughing. But now everything has changed, and Christmas is no longer like it used to be.

My mother wipes the tears from her eyes, gets up and walks to her bed, and reaching under the pillow, pulls out two small packages wrapped in brown paper. She hands one to me and the other to my sister. Quickly, we open our packages, and I discover a pair of colorful mittens. My sister finds the same. My mother tells us that she was given the wool and needles by the Müller grandmother, and she has been knitting in secret for weeks. We both thank her for the present, and I am now aware that no matter what has happened to us—Christmas still exists. I finish my glass of wine, lie down on my bed, and fall asleep.

I am awakened by a dim light coming into our room and soft voices coming from the table. I see my parents sitting in the dim light, and get up and join them. I sense that there was something different about the night before, and then realize that there were no bombers overhead, or the usual sirens. I ask my parents if this is true, and my mother tells me that on this Christmas night the world was at peace—even if for a very short time.

The week before the new year of 1945 goes very fast. There are the usual air raids, but we have no school, and when New Year's Eve arrives, we all go to the Gasthaus. We eat soup, and I, again, am given a half glass of beer by the kind bartender. The rest of the night goes without any celebration, and again, I sleep through the night without sirens.

I don't know if the silence is because of Christmas, or the sky being heavily overcast. Sometimes, if the sky is cloudy, there are no planes overhead. One of my friends at school explained that if it rains, and the clouds are heavy overhead, there are no raids because targets on the ground cannot be seen from the sky above where the planes fly. This is good.

Sometime in the middle of January, when we are in our room, there is a knock on the door. As the door opens, there stands a man in a uniform. He hands my father something that looks like a letter, explaining that he is delivering a telegram sent by the German army.

After the man leaves, my father opens it, and at once begins to read. In no time, I hear the German word, "tod," and I immediately know that someone is dead. My father's voice becomes weak, and he tells us that Valdo, my cousin, has been killed on the Eastern Front. My mother begins to cry, and before I know it, we are all crying.

Eventually, the crying stops, and my father suggests that we go to the Gasthaus. We all put on coats and leave in a hurry. Once we are seated, the waitress comes over and asks for our order. She sees my mother trying to control her tears, and asks her what is wrong.

My mother explains, and the waitress puts her arms around her and tries to comfort her. When she returns with our order, my father reaches into his coat pocket for money. The waitress tells him that he does not have to pay. As we finish our beers in silence, some of the guests in the Gasthaus come to our table and express their sorrow. It seems that most of them have a family member in the army, and hope that someday they will not be receiving a telegram.

After finishing our beer, we leave, and return to the Müller Farm and our room. My parents wonder if there is a way of notifying our relatives, but that is impossible. Valdo's parents and sister are in Siberia, and the other relatives, including his brother Uno, and our grandparents, have by now been taken over by the Russians, who are advancing further and further into the West.

So much is happening—and quickly. We must always be alert, I think.

Chapter 37.

EARLY 1945 TO END OF WAR IN GRAITSCHEN

As time goes by, we hear rumors that the Western Front, driven by Americans and British, is also advancing. My father tells me that he, along with most, hope the Western Front will reach us before the Russian army that is advancing from the East. He tells us if there is a chance that the Russians will come first, we will have to again flee—but to the West.

When I discuss the war with my friends in school, they seem to think everyone prefers that the Allies reach Graitschen before the Russians. But at the same time, they think that Germany will still win the war.

When I hear this, I think back to the comments a German naval officer made to my mother on the Moltkefels, when he heard that we were planning to stay near Berlin. He told my mother that he felt the war was lost, and we should go as far west as possible. In any case, the approaching two fronts become a daily concern. Which front, we wonder, will reach us first?

We are well into January. The weather is colder, and we sometimes wake up in the morning and see snow covering the earth. As I think back to our winters in Estonia, I remember snowstorms that covered everything, and of how my grandfather would hitch one horse to a sleigh to ride to the nearest village to buy needed products, or food they did not grow on the farm.

Before I know it, we are into February, and the sun is beginning to feel warm. In the middle of February, we hear rumors that the city of Dresden, which is about 150 kilometers to our east, has been bombed two nights in a row. The Allied bombers have dropped bombs that apparently set everything on fire, and with the city burning, thousands of people have died. Some, we hear, were running through the streets on fire—like burning candles. Everyone is talking about this horror.

Also, with the coming of spring, the air raids seem to increase. One day, while we are in the basement waiting for the air raid to pass, we hear a plane low overhead, and a loud whistling sound, followed by a loud explosion which hurts our ears.

After the sirens sound to announce the end of the raid, we rush outside. Herr Müller is wearing his metal helmet. We see a large crater in the ground across the road from the Müller Farm entrance. There are large pieces of ground and parts of the street thrown all over. We realize that a bomb has hit the village.

As soon as possible, I am in the street watching some men fill the hole with shovels. Without warning, we see a man in the distance, walking and staggering toward us. As he gets closer to us, he raises his arms. The men filling the crater immediately drop their shovels, and run over to him. They can see he is an American pilot. Most likely, his plane crashed after he dropped the bomb on our village. I think he must have parachuted some distance from the village, and now needs help.

After a fast discussion, the men decide to take him to Bürgel. One of the men leaves, and soon returns with his tractor, which is pulling a wagon. The rest of us stay with the pilot while he is doing this. The tractor driver asks me to ride along. I don't know why. But I quickly agree to go along. The men put the injured pilot on the wagon, and several men sit near him. During the ride he speaks a few words in English, but none of us is able to understand what he is trying to say.

After a short ride, we arrive in Bürgel, where we see some German army troops standing near a truck. The man with the tractor stops, and explains what has happened, and the soldiers carefully place the pilot on the back of their truck. The soldiers tell us that he is now a prisoner who is injured, and that they will take him to a hospital.

After this, we leave and return to Graitschen. No one talks during the ride. I notice that in the Gasthaus and elsewhere, adults do not talk about the war and how it is going. With the exception of the horror of Dresden. I remember seeing a sign when we were in Bürgel. It was a picture of a man with his forefinger on his closed lips, with the words, "Shhh! The enemy is listening." Adults only talk about family members being in the war, and of how they hope they are safe. Or they talk about everyday things, like the weather. I think this is because of the sign that says, "Shhh!" And it is why nobody talks as we ride home on the wagon, after delivering the injured American pilot.

When I get back to the Müller Farm, I explain to my parents what happened, and they do not seem to be upset because I did not tell them I was leaving the village with the men. I think they are so relieved that the bomb did not hit anyone, that they forget to be angry with me.

When I ask my father, he explains that most likely the plane was hit by anti-aircraft guns over Jena, which has military significance, especially, compared to our farm village. And once the pilot knew that he was going to crash, he had to drop the bomb, because if he could not parachute off the plane in time, he would be killed when the plane crashed and the bomb exploded. My father also says that, in this case, the pilot is lucky to have been able to parachute before the crash.

The next day, there are also American fighter planes to worry about. They are much smaller than the bombers we have become used to. The fighter planes appear suddenly, out of nowhere, and sometimes fly low over a road that leads into Graitschen. They usually appear, as my friends have warned me, when there are German army trucks traveling on the highway. And sometimes, when they fire their machine guns, an explosion can be heard, meaning that the truck has been hit.

Often, the German soldiers traveling on the trucks appear in our village later, and this means that when they heard a low flying plane approaching, they jumped from the trucks and ran fast into a field or trees, and then threw themselves on the ground and waited until the raid passed.

After awhile, I notice that sometimes the trucks change their travel times to night and drive through the village with their lights turned off.

Because the Allies are approaching from the West, and the Russians from the East, my father one day tells me that he would like to go to a forest behind the Müller Farm, which is at least a fifteen-minute walk away. He thinks that if the Allies are approaching the village, and there is resistance by the German troops, the village could easily be bombed from the air, or attacked by the advancing artillery and tanks. In that case, we would have to flee into the forest.

My father and I visit the forest the next day. As we enter the forest and continue walking, we eventually come to a formation of rocks that hides a small cave. He tells me this is where we will flee, if necessary. He adds that we should return here soon, when the Front is nearer, and hide some food and water in metal containers.

At this point, we return to the Müller Farm and discuss our plan with my mother. We decide to set aside some food, such as mashed potatoes mixed with lard, and some containers of water. We will take these to the cave a few days before the Front is expected to reach us. Then, when the time is right, we will all go to the cave, taking along blankets and enough matches—in case we have to build a small fire out of dead branches, to keep us warm if the weather is cold at night.

If, however, the Eastern Front reaches us first, we will have to be prepared to flee on foot toward the West and the Allies, because being caught by the Russians will mean a forced return to Estonia, and most likely, beyond—to Siberia or any other labor camp.

All this activity chases away my boredom, but brings with it an alarm for what may be coming.

In the beginning of March, my parents receive a letter from one of Valdo's fellow soldiers on the Eastern Front. He writes that Valdo was shot by the advancing troops, while he was removing the boots of a dead soldier, because his own boots were worn. The fellow soldier does not identify the advancing troops, nor does he mention the country where this happened. This information seems to add to the sadness we felt when the telegram arrived a few weeks earlier.

School continues. One day in school, the teacher announces that all of us who are twelve years of age, or over, are expected to join the Hitler Youth. He says that someone from the German army will be visiting the village, and we will be told when he is here.

I am relieved that I am only ten, a few days from my eleventh birthday, on March 16, but still too young to be expected to join. I know of no one who wants to join. But no one can refuse. A few days later, some boys in school tell me that they will be given some training, in the near future. But they do not expect to be sent to either of the advancing fronts.

My father wants to walk to the cave with me, to make sure it is still empty. We start shortly after lunch, and as we reach the middle of the field on our way to the forest, we hear planes flying very low overhead. My father shouts for me to lie down on the ground, and he quickly drops on top of me.

We hear machine gun fire and bombs exploding in the direction of the highway. As the planes disappear, we cautiously get up and see a convoy of German army trucks speeding down the road. But some are stopped, with smoke and flames rising above them. The planes disappear, and we run toward the forest. Once there, we look in the cave, and we see that it is still empty.

We leave, but before entering the open field beyond the forest, we listen for the noise of planes. There is no aircraft noise, and we run across the field and back to the Müller Farm.

My father explains that the reason he made me lie down, and then dropped on top of me, was to conceal our presence from the pilots flying over us. Rather than the pilots seeing two moving objects, which they may have decided to fire upon, they saw only one unmoving object.

I feel lucky that my father always seems to be prepared, and thinking ahead.

At this time, my sister starts complaining about pain in one of her legs. Because the pain does not go away after a few days, my parents decide they must take her to see a doctor in Jena, which is about seven kilometers away. One morning, we leave, and walk to Jena. My father and mother take turns carrying her, and we arrive in Jena in a couple of hours, after sitting down along the road to rest, sometimes.

The clinic we go to is across from the Jena railroad station, in a concrete building that is shaped like a pyramid. I have never seen a building shaped like this, and my father explains that it is, actually, an above ground air shelter. If a bomb is dropped from a plane, it glances off as it explodes, rather than entering the building through the roof, where it could explode inside, cause great damage, and kill many people. I think this pyramid building is a wonderful idea.

While my sister is being seen by a doctor, air raid sirens begin to howl, and we can hear exploding bombs. We remain inside until the raid is over, and the all-clear siren sounds. As we leave the building, we see several bomb craters, nearby, which were not there when we entered.

On the walk back to Graitschen, my parents tell me that the doctor gave them some medicine to take away my sister's pain. They say the condition that has slowed the growth of her leg, and given her pain, will disappear. I can see that my parents are greatly relieved, as they take turns carrying my sister back to Graitschen. The bigger threat of bombs in Jena, a factory city, makes us hurry as quickly as possible to our small farming village of Graitschen.

The middle of March arrives, and it is my birthday. We all go to the Gasthaus to celebrate, and my mother whispers something into the waitress's ear. After we have finished our soup, the waitress brings me a large, flat piece of cake, covered with plums and a creamy white sauce. It is beautiful, and I happily thank my parents. I give my sister part of it, because it will, also, be her birthday in only one week. I eat my portion slowly, trying to make the sweet taste last for a long time. My parents tell me that there are no presents for my birthday, blaming it on the war. But I tell them it is still a good birthday.

As we reach the last days of March, we hear rumors that the Allies have crossed the Rhine River, somewhere near the city of Mainz. My father tells us that the crossing is less than one hundred kilometers to our northwest.

He also says that we do not know where the Eastern Front is at this time. However, if the Russians have occupied Poland, they could be about 150 kilometers to our east. Then again, if they are well into Czechoslovakia, they could be much closer. I feel the wonder and worry increase daily. We are always on the alert. But school continues.

With April comes spring, and the weather is much warmer. There is green on the trees, and flowers are blooming. With every day, it is rumored that the Western Front is getting closer. Great, good news.

There is much movement of German soldiers. Some of the troops on trucks are heading east, and some are going west. We all hope that most of the troop movement will be to the east, which would mean that the Eastern Front can be held in place longer—and the Allies can reach us first.

In the second week of April, we begin to hear the sound of artillery to the west. Finally, there is no school. The people in Graitschen feel that in a few days the Allied tanks will reach us, which is good news.

On April 12, we hear continual artillery explosions, and some bursts are close to the village. In the evening, Herr Müller tells us to go into the basement. When we arrive, the basement is full of villagers, who apparently have no basement of their own.

Herr Müller tells us persons in authority have announced the village will display a white flag, at the western end of the village, where the Americans are advancing, and warns that no one is allowed to resist the approaching tanks with any firearms, such as, anti-tank bazookas or machine guns.

He, especially, makes this clear to two Hitler Youth members who are present. Everyone agrees with Herr Müller's judgment. Because if there is any resistance from anyone, after the advancing tank crews have seen the white flag, they will pull back and bomb the village, which obviously would lead to many villagers being killed.

After Herr Müller has spoken, we prepare ourselves for a long wait. The intervals of silence are interrupted by artillery explosions, which are getting louder as the night goes on. People sit without speaking. My mother has brought along some slices of rye bread covered with lard and mashed potatoes. I think these are the provisions we set aside for our cave, in case the Russians got here first.

As the long night passes, and early daylight arrives, there are still some artillery explosions. But they have become fewer. Sometime around nine in the morning, there is total silence. Then abruptly, we can hear a different sound—a rumbling noise—occasionally interrupted by screeching sounds. Some people in the basement definitely agree that tanks have arrived in the village. After a short while, this sound stops. And again—there is silence.

At this time, Herr Müller approaches my father, and asks him to leave the basement and try to attract the attention of the American troops who have now arrived. I know this is dangerous. What if they think he is going to offer resistance? However, my father exits the basement, and steps into the yard with his arms upraised. Swiftly, two soldiers approach him. They have their weapons at an angle—pointing at my father. They silently motion for him to return into the basement.

When he does as ordered, one soldier quickly follows him down the steps. The other descends the stairs backward, keeping an eye on the top entrance. I rush to the bottom of the stairs where my father is now standing, because I am so relieved that he was not shot.

The soldier motions with his rifle for everyone to exit. Quickly, without speaking, we do as we are told. One soldier remains in the basement, and the other is at the top, motioning for all of us to enter the yard and to stand in a group.

By now, other soldiers have arrived in the yard. They all look at our group of people, and we remain motionless and silent, as these soldiers walk past the men, touching their chest area and pockets. They do the same with the two members of the Hitler Youth.

The soldiers motion to us to leave the yard, and walk to the street. We remain huddled at the gate that opens to the street. Suddenly, I push ahead of the adults, in order to see the entire street. I see that it is filled with tanks, with soldiers sitting on top of them, their weapons pointing toward the ground, or upward toward the sky.

My parents and my sister join me, and my father says that we have been saved—by the Americans. My mother then speaks, and reminds us that today is her birthday, and then she tells us that what has happened today is, in fact, the most wonderful birthday present. It is April 13, 1945.

My mother then sinks to the ground, and embraces my sister and me, holding us tight. It is then that I notice tears in her eyes. I try to fight back tears. But I can't. And I, along with my sister, begin to cry. My mother tells us, when we cry today, we are not sad—we are happy.

Before long, the tanks begin to rumble up the street, and this, again, catches our attention. Suddenly, we hear a shot from up the street, in the direction of where the tanks are moving. Shortly after the shot is heard, a woman runs into the street, screaming. I soon learn that a boy whom I knew, whose father is on the Eastern Front, had been watching the tanks from behind a curtain covering a second floor window. His face was partly visible. The curtain moved, and a soldier on a tank viewed the movement as a threat. The soldier fired a single shot at the window. I hear that the boy was killed instantly. After that—the adults say—his mother lost her mind.

Eventually, we are all allowed to return to our homes. At night, I listen to the Allied bombers overhead, but they keep going, and there are no air raid sirens. Some of the other Estonian refugees come over to our room at the Müller Farm. The adults all celebrate by drinking lots of wine, and I sleep well for the first time in weeks.

The next morning, I awake before my parents and my sister, drink all the wine remaining in glasses, and feel good.

Chapter 38.

DISPLACED PERSONS CAMP IN JENA

Everything is different when the Americans arrive. For us, in Graitschen, the war has ended. There are bombers overhead, but they are going beyond us. There are American soldiers in the village, and they ride around in trucks. Occasionally, many trucks pass through the village hauling supplies and soldiers. The Americans all live in a large building in town, and they wave when they drive past people walking along the street. We wave back.

School has started, again, but we no longer have to do the salute with our right arm extended to the front and slightly above our shoulder. I still don't care for school, but I have to attend because my parents, for some reason, insist on it.

There is a greater shortage of food, because the store distributing rations has been closed. We are told that the German money is worthless, but we are able to exchange small Russian gold coins for food at the Gasthaus. My mother tells me that she expected this, and hid some coins inside the lining of her coat before leaving Estonia.

When we give a coin to the woman serving food at the Gasthaus, she takes it, and writes on a piece of paper how many more meals we will receive. My parents then know when it's time to bring along another gold coin. My father says that without these gold coins, we would be very hungry.

Meals at the Gasthaus are always steaming vegetable soup and a slice of rye bread. Of course, there is always the half glass of beer that I am given. This seems to take the place of a dessert, which I would have received in Estonia, and it satisfies me.

Weeks pass. One day, my parents receive instructions from two American soldiers who come to the farm one day. We are required to go to the building occupied by the Americans, and we are told what will happen to us. Although my parents speak no English, one of the soldiers speaks German. He tells us that the war is almost over for everyone, and when it ends, the refugees will be shipped to other locations. My father asks the soldiers if we will be sent back to Estonia—now occupied by the Russians. The soldiers tell him that this will not happen. We are very relieved to hear we will not have to worry about this danger any longer.

One day, while we are at the Gasthaus, the woman bringing the food tells us that Berlin has been taken over by the Russians. She says that the Americans have nearly reached an area close to Berlin. We are hoping my mother's distant relative, near Berlin, will be safe. Ever since Graitschen has become occupied by Americans, it seems all right to talk openly about the Eastern Front, and so she adds that we are very lucky that the Russian Front did not reach us before the American tanks arrived on April 13. We know this.

May arrives, and the weather is warm. We help Herr Müller with work in his vineyards, such as, hoeing the ground around the grape plants. For this, we are rewarded with sausage sandwiches and slices of plum cake. This is wonderful, because the ration store has not reopened.

About a week into May, word spreads that Germany has surrendered. The war is over for everyone! I am now eleven years old, and my sister is eight years old. It seems this is the first time in our lives that we have not known war. Everyone feels cheered when they hear this news. What a relief. We are encouraged.

As the end of May nears, two more American soldiers visit to inform us that in a few days, all the refugees from the East will be moved to a camp in Jena. Their visit is followed by a notice that in two days, we will be picked up with a truck and taken to Jena.

My mother hurries to pack our two suitcases, our backpack, and the small red suitcase, in preparation. On the morning of our departure, we bid farewell to the Müller family, and my parents and my sister and

I thank them for providing us with a place to live, along with much-needed food. They give my father their address, but we have none to give them.

In a little while, a truck arrives with two American soldiers. A few people are already on the truck, and after a few more stops to pick up more refugees, the driver heads for Jena. In a short time, we arrive at some older two-story buildings, which were part of a German army base.

We are asked to get off the truck, and one of the soldiers directs us into a building, where other people are already gathered outside a large room. The soldiers tell us that twenty-eight of us will occupy this room, and others, as they enter the building, are told to walk up the hallway and go into other rooms.

One side of the room we enter is filled with twenty-eight mattresses. They are placed side by side, from one end of the room to the other. The floor is completely covered, so there is little walking space. As my father enters the room, he places our suitcases on the first four mattresses next to the door. He holds onto his briefcase from Estonia, which I notice he carries—everywhere.

Once all the mattresses have been taken, we are instructed to go back into the hallway, where a soldier speaks to us in German. He describes another building, in which we will receive food three times a day. We are told we will be housed in this building for, possibly, one week, while other buildings are prepared to allow each family to have its own room, or share one with another family.

As I return to our room, I wonder if our situation is actually becoming worse. Someone says there will be thousands of people in this camp. I hear my father say there are people here from most of the Eastern European countries and from the Baltic countries. I immediately miss the village of Graitschen, where we lived in a room on the Müller Farm and had the whole room to ourselves. I think of the friendly man behind the counter at the Gasthaus, who always gave me a half glass of beer, and I wonder if that life will ever return.

I sit on my mattress and look around. The room is full of people, most standing up, and none of them seem to know what to do next. I wander outside and then back in again, not really knowing what to do. We have nothing to do.

The meals we eat are soup and rye bread. About the same as we had on the Moltkefels while we were crossing the Baltic Sea. Sleeping in this room filled with twenty-eight people again reminds me of the Moltkefels. The war has ended. But has my life changed for the better? However, there are no air raids. There are no bombs dropping. We have food.

As the days pass, I meet some boys my age from Estonia. We do not have school, which I think is one good thing, so we spend the days wandering the camp area between meals. After breakfast, we wander. After lunch, we wander. After supper, we wander until we go to bed. My sister stays with my parents.

One day, as my friends and I wander along a railroad track, near where our food is served, we discover parts of a destroyed train. We find the wheels that belonged to a freight car, and without discussion, we begin moving the heavy set of iron wheels from the side of the track onto the track. Before we know it, the set of wheels is on the track, and we begin to push it along.

As the set of wheels begins to roll, it picks up speed, and we then notice the track is missing some distance away. And people are crossing over the missing track, on a path to the food building. The heavy, runaway iron wheels, are heading right for them.

I look around, but my friends have disappeared. I start running after the rolling wheels, trying to stop them before they reach people who are crossing. I reach the broken area of the track, just ahead of the wheels. But I see that I cannot stop them. I scream, and as people look toward me, they scatter. The heavy wheels roll off the track and land in the path. I am relieved that no one has been hit. I stop near the path, to catch my breath.

But, before I am able to leave, a man in an army uniform takes hold of my arm, turns me around, and beats me across my back with a stiff leather whip. While he is doing this, he screams in a language I cannot understand. After several more lashes, he releases my arm, and I run off, never looking back.

When I meet my friends later, I tell them what happened. To my surprise, none of them show any reaction to my story. But, from there on, they all seem to consider me as the leader of our small group. And I make sure my parents do not hear about the runaway wheels.

Time goes by, and we are moved into small rooms. One family to each room. We now have narrow beds with a thin mattress to sleep on. This is good, I think.

Sometime in early summer, rumors circulate that the area of Germany we live in will be given to the Russian army, and we all know, if this true, we have to leave and head west. We keep our bags ready, because my father says we may have to leave on a moment's notice. We hear that the Russian occupying army can easily reach us in a day. Now all we can do is wait. And worry.

One day, we are all told that we can leave the camp area during the daytime, but will have to return in the evening. However, my father warns my sister and me to stay close to the building where we live, so if he decides it is time to leave, we can go quickly. We know that wherever we go, we will have to walk and carry our belongings.

A few weeks later, we are still here in Jena. We are now told that the camp full of refugees will be evacuated, to the west. We will be going to a new location in Germany, which will be beyond the area to be turned over to the Russian army. We are, again, greatly relieved that we will be beyond the Russians, and we are cheered that we will not have to travel on foot. Now it is a matter of waiting for an order to leave.

After a few days, we are notified by a young woman from Estonia, who speaks some English, that we will be leaving the following day, on

American army trucks. It seems people in our building will be the first to be moved, and our destination will be Wiesbaden. My father says it is about 250 kilometers to our southwest.

The next morning, we are told we will be leaving that afternoon, and we should be ready. We are ready. After lunch, everyone from our building gathers outside the building, with their bags packed. We wait.

Chapter 39.

DP CAMP IN WIESBADEN

Sometime late in the afternoon, an open American army truck, with two Negro drivers, pulls up to our building. This is the first time I have ever seen Negroes, outside of geography books, because we do not have Negroes in Estonia. They look like any other soldiers, but darker. The lady who speaks English instructs us to climb on the truck.

We are seated on the wooden benches, along each side of the truck, and once those seats are filled, I, along with some others, sit on the floor. Quickly glancing at the people on the truck, I see that there are twenty-eight people with their luggage. They fill the entire truck. The female interpreter climbs into the front, sits between the two drivers, and without a warning, the truck moves, picking up speed.

Because I am sitting right behind the drivers and the young woman, I decide to stand up so that I can get a better view of the road ahead. The truck picks up more speed, and I look around as we pass through the streets of Jena. Wherever I look, I see buildings that are destroyed by bombs. I now understand what happened during each air raid, when the planes flew over Graitschen, toward Jena.

I see men and women bent over removing bricks and pieces of wood from the rubble, where once a building stood. I wonder if they are looking for items that were once part of their house. Or are they looking for people, perhaps relatives who lived there, but now are dead and buried by piles of bricks? I finally know that we are lucky to have lived in small Graitschen, and to have escaped being buried alive in Jena.

We leave the city, and follow an open road. Sometimes, the truck slows, and we leave the highway and drive around large craters, in the middle of the road, which have been left by a bomb.

As we travel on, I see columns of people walking along the highway. Some are pushing carts, or pulling small wagons filled with bags of belongings. Some of the walkers are carrying small children. They are all heading away from the Russian army which will soon be coming. As we pass these columns of sad, tired people, I hope they all will reach a safe place—wherever that may be.

As the truck drives on, it begins to rain. People huddle on the floor of the truck, trying to protect themselves from the pouring rain by covering up with extra clothes. I do likewise, but once the rain stops, I again stand up behind the truck cab, trying to see what is ahead.

Our travel is slow, because the truck often comes to a stop, then slowly moves around bombed highway bridges or large bomb craters. Sometimes, the truck stops for a long time, waiting in line as convoys of trucks take their time driving around these obstructions.

Before I know it, evening arrives. After about an hour of driving through the early night, we enter a city. The interpreter turns around in her seat and tells some of us, through the open cab, that we have reached Wiesbaden, our destination.

The word spreads quickly from one passenger to the next. Some of the riders stand up and try to catch sight of our new home. As I look around in the semidarkness, I again see a city ruined by bombs from the air. There are no buildings with lights on, and it is a scene of awful destruction. Like Jena.

Eventually, the truck pulls up to a tall wire fence with a gate. In front of it, a large sign says, "DP Camp 563." Two soldiers approach the truck and speak to the driver, who then drives through the gate and stops, eventually, near a group of grey buildings. We are told that we have arrived in a former German army camp, and we should all climb off the truck. I jump off, and my father helps my mother and sister get off.

When we are off the truck, our interpreter speaks to several soldiers, who then point toward a large stone building. It has four stories with several chimneys and many windows. Built out of stone, it looks like a castle to me. At the front, I see an American flag lighted by an electric light that shines up the flagpole. We are huddled and wet and tired and quiet, but I now feel that we have finally reached a place that is safe from the Russian army.

Several men, including my father, go into the building and come out a short while later. They tell us that the large room, which has been assigned to the people from our truck, is filthy. Whoever occupied this room before our arrival used it as a bathroom while they lived in it.

The American soldiers decide to look at the room themselves, and they return quickly, holding their hands over their faces. They speak to the interpreter, and we are told to remain outside until we are given materials and equipment for cleaning the room.

A short while later, the soldiers deliver buckets and brooms, as well as a shovel. The men, and a few women, return to the room and begin to clean. My mother keeps my sister outside, but I follow the cleaners. As I look into the room, I realize that it will be a long time before we can enter the room for the night.

While we stand outside, a convoy of American army trucks begins to leave the fenced camp. They are filled with men and women, and as they pass us, they yell in a language I cannot understand. My mother, who understands Russian, tells me that these are Russian prisoners who are returning East, and they are cursing and swearing at our group. She is glad we do not have to share this camp the Americans have established with the type of people who are just leaving. My mother also says that, if this group is returning to Russia, they will not be treated kindly, because the Russians feel that anyone who has allowed himself or herself to be captured by the enemy is a coward, and they will probably be killed or sent to a labor camp in Siberia. I wonder if these people are the ones who used our future home as a bathroom.

As we wait for the room to be cleaned, an American soldier comes up to us, and through our young interpreter, says to follow him so that we can be given food. We are all thankful to follow the soldier and go into a large room in a nearby building. As we enter, I see long tables and benches. We are directed to an area to the side, where a long table is filled with large kettles of steaming soup and containers of bread. We are instructed to pick up a metal container and a spoon. Just like on the Moltkefels.

Behind the longest table are several American soldiers wearing white aprons. As we pass them, they fill our containers with steaming soup. The man at the end hands us two slices of bread. The bread is white. It's the type we used to eat in Estonia on holidays and Sundays. My mother and sister follow behind, and we sit down at one of the long tables.

I immediately dip my spoon into the soup, and as I raise it to my mouth, I see that this soup has pieces of meat in it. I quickly eat the soup and take large bites out of the white bread. This bread tastes as good as my grandmother's Sunday bread.

Before I know it, I have finished. As I wait for my mother and sister to finish, a soldier taps me on my shoulder and points toward the soup kettle still standing on the table. He also points his hand to his mouth, and I quickly see this is an invitation for me to get more food. I nod my head and smile in his direction as I hurry to get up from the table. Nodding is the only gesture I can think of which will show my feeling of thanks. As I eat my soup and the tasty white bread, I see the other diners returning to the soup and bread table. We eat—but nobody speaks.

Before our group leaves the dining room, the men and women who have been cleaning our sleeping room arrive, and fall in line for the soup with meat and the white bread. My father sits down, and as he begins to eat, he tells us that the filthy rooms had been occupied by Russians who, apparently, intentionally created the filth and dirt. When the Russian army occupied Estonia in the fall of 1940, he adds, many of the soldiers had never seen a toilet and would wash their face in one. I am very glad they are gone.

After finishing our meal, we all return to the building that is our new home. When we arrive, I see men carrying in beds made out of metal, which they are placing one on top of the other. Next come mattresses, and before long, we are invited to enter with our belongings. The four in our family settle on four beds placed at the end of the room. My parents tell my sister and me that we will be sleeping on the top beds.

This is the first time in my life that I will be sleeping up in the air. We do not have pillows, but we are each given two dark green woolen blankets. As people get organized, I count the beds, and there are exactly twenty-eight of them. The room does not seem to be as crowded as the one in Jena, because we are now sleeping on top of each other. The room has a strong odor, and my father explains that it was necessary to clean it with strong soaps.

Before long, everyone is asleep, and I sleep very well up in the air. I cannot wait until morning to find out what lies ahead. I awaken early.

We are instructed to go for breakfast where we ate the night before. Breakfast is white bread and oatmeal, cooked and given out in large amounts. The oatmeal is just the same as in Estonia, and I like it—especially with the sugar on top.

We are, also, given a daily meal schedule, and told where to go if we become sick. They tell us that the crowded room, which is our home now, is only temporary. In about two weeks, we will be moved into smaller rooms in another building, with two families to a room. In a few months, we will probably be relocated to another camp, which will result in each nationality group occupying its own camp. I remember overhearing my father say that there are people from the Eastern countries and the Baltics here, too. Just like in Jena, there are several thousand people here. Before we leave the dining area, we are also advised that, very shortly, we will be allowed to leave the camp for the day and go into the city of Wiesbaden.

So, a few days later, my parents suggest I take along my sister and visit the town of Wiesbaden, which surrounds the camp. I leave with her, after breakfast, and we walk for about half-an-hour, and arrive in the center of town. There are many, many bomb-damaged buildings.

As we pass one where workers are digging and removing fallen debris, I immediately detect a strange odor, and my sister covers her nose with both her hands. I notice that each man digging has a handkerchief tied over his nose and mouth. When I approach, with my sister some distance behind, I see a sheet spread over something, and as I get closer, I see a hand sticking out from under the cloth. I now know that what I am seeing is what is done after a war is over. The dead have to be dug out and then reburied. The strong, sweet odor of the dead is the smell that follows the end of war. My sister does not come any closer. Once again, I am very grateful that something like this has not happened to me, or my family.

As my sister and I start our walk back to camp, we pass a row of army trucks stopped along a street. The truck cabs do not have doors or windows, and there are two soldiers sitting in each cab. As we pass one truck, a soldier waves at us and motions for us to come to him. When we come closer, he gets out of the cab, walks to my sister, picks her up, and holds her tightly in his arms. He says the word "daughter." I immediately know what he is saying. The word daughter sounds like the German word "tochter." But he is speaking English. I nod my head, and I know he has a daughter who must look like my sister. As he places my sister on the ground, I see sadness in his eyes, and then I see tears dropping from the corners of his eyes.

He reaches into his pocket and takes out a small package wrapped in brown paper. He opens it. It looks like a bar of chocolate, like we had in the stores in Estonia. He breaks off a piece and hands it to me. I nod my head in thanks. He then hands the remainder to my sister, who smiles. As the column of trucks begins to move, he jumps into the cab of the truck. As they slowly pull away, he turns around and waves, and we do the same.

My sister and I leave, and return to camp. We have not had chocolate since we left Estonia. But my sister wants to share the candy with our parents, so she will not give me another piece.

When we arrive in camp it's time for the noon meal. We gather in line, and I notice new people. My parents know a man in the group, who tells us about a man who killed himself with soup. This soup-man had not had any food for a long time, and when he arrived at a refugee camp, and was fed soup, he continued to eat until his stomach burst, and he died. This story scares me into not eating too much at once.

Days pass slowly because there is very little to do, other than walk to the center of Wiesbaden. Although I usually take along my sister, I have met some boys from Estonia, and we exchange stories about our escape. Theirs are similar to mine—pretty scary.

My mother accepts a volunteer job at the DP camp clinic. She seems to enjoy it, and says she has always wanted to be a nurse. I think she is good at this work, because she knew what to do when I ate too many plums at the Müller Farm.

As time goes on, we are moved into another stone building and into rooms that house fewer people. At first, we share a room with another family from Viljandi whom my parents know, a doctor and his wife, along with their son and daughter. Surprisingly, the daughter is the one who has been our interpreter. I wonder if she has learned to speak English at the University of Tartu, the school my father graduated from when he was a young man.

Eventually, we are given a room of our own in a former army barracks, with the bathrooms at the end of each floor. The rooms have no cooking stoves or sinks, and we continue to eat our soup in the dining area where we ate when we first arrived. To keep clean, our family goes to a large public bathhouse in Wiesbaden once a week. It has warm water from a natural spring. We all look forward to this Saturday treat.

One day, when we are gathered for a meal, the young interpreter tells us a story. After everyone has finished eating, she stands in front of the group and tells us that if any of us go to the center of Wiesbaden, especially the younger people, we should be aware that someone may approach us with a package. This person, usually older, will ask us to take the package upstairs into a building for them, because they are old and cannot climb the stairs. If we agree to do as asked, we will never be seen again. Once we are upstairs in the building, we will be killed—and our body will be made into sausage—which will then be sold on the black market.

As soon as the interpreter is finished, my mother looks at me and asks me if I have paid attention. I immediately tell her that I have and assure her that I will be careful. I do not want her to doubt me, and then, possibly, not allow me to leave the camp. However, the warning really does not scare me, because I think that something like that will not happen to me. Maybe it could happen to someone else, but not to me.

One day, two of my friends and I, while walking around the central part of Wiesbaden, see people entering a Gasthaus. I tell my friends about the friendly man in the Graitschen Gasthaus who gave me a half glass of beer, and suggest that maybe the same can happen here. I have some money in a leather money pouch which my father has recently given me. After some discussion, we agree to go in. When we walk inside, the man behind the bar sees us and begins to yell, telling us to get out. He waves in our direction, motioning with his hand toward the door. We all turn around and run out. Once outside, I wonder about the kindly man in Graitschen who always welcomed me, and I wish that I was again back there in the friendly farm village we left after the Americans arrived.

Another day, my friends tell me they heard that a girl, a little older than we are, went to Wiesbaden from the camp and never returned. The American soldiers from the camp searched for her, but they did not find her. My friends and I think that maybe she forgot the warning we were given a while ago, about taking a package to someone, and then got killed. We say we will never forget.

At the end of July, 1945, we are advised that there is no chance Russia will withdraw from lands that were once independent, including Estonia, Latvia, and Lithuania. According to my parents, this eliminates any chance we can return to Estonia. My father says the Russians are continually trying to get the Allies to send refugees back to their homelands. We are worried, but we eventually learn this will not happen, because people are being given the choice of returning voluntarily. No one will return, because everyone knows such a move would result in their being sent to Siberian labor camps, where their friends and relatives were taken during the Russian occupation.

We can't help but think we will never see my grandparents and other relatives again. We feel sad and hopeless as we become aware of this awful truth—which we try not to think about all the time.

Now that we know the Russians will not leave Estonia, and we cannot return, our stay in Germany seems to be permanent. As a result, the Americans in charge of the camps are beginning to make plans for our future. One of the plans is to set up schools. My parents tell me that every nationality in the camp will have its own school. Former teachers in the camp are being asked to come forward and work on starting these schools. For me, this is bad news. I do not look forward to school here—or anywhere. But I think my sister does, although, I cannot imagine why.

Summer is passing, and the weather is now very warm as we enter August. One day, there is an announcement that we will receive clothes which have been sent to Germany from people in America. My mother goes to be given the clothes for our family. The short-sleeved shirt and short pants I am given are a very welcome addition to the double layer of clothes I have had to wear, although not all at once, since we left Estonia. Especially, in this warm weather, these clothes are welcome.

One day, my friends and I decide to walk to the Rhine River, which is at the edge of Wiesbaden. My mother tells me to take my sister along, but warns me that she should not go near the water, because she could easily fall in. Walking to the outskirts of Wiesbaden takes us about half-an-hour, and suddenly, there is the Rhine.

As I look before me, I see a bombed-out bridge crossing the river, and beyond, in the distance, is the city of Mainz. I remember my father telling me that this is where the American army crossed the Rhine. As I continue looking, I hear my sister scream.

I run to her, and I see her crying, and pointing at an object that is partly submerged in the river. As my friends and I gather near her, we can see the body of a man lying face up in the water. His eyes are open, but he is not moving. He is covered by dirt and grass, and he slowly moves back and forth as the small waves from the river hit his body.

My sister's screaming has attracted several adults. After viewing the dead body, a woman takes my sister's hand and leads her away from the river. Several men tell us to move away, as some of them approach the body and bend over it. My friends and I decide to take my sister and return to the camp. We have seen enough, and they won't let us get closer, anyway.

On our way back, I think of the man and the war that has ended—and of how there are still these reminders of the war.

When we return to the camp, I explain to my mother what has happened. She talks to my sister, who still seems to be excited after having seen a person who is dead—and still moving.

Before I know it, we are told that school will start in early September. Students are ordered to gather in a large building one day. The teachers are there, and we are seen, one at a time, with a parent present. I quickly find myself assigned to grade five. The classes I am given include Religion, History, Mathematics, Natural Science, Geography, Drawing, Calligraphy, Manual Instruction, Gymnastics, and Singing, along with the Languages of Estonian, English, and German.

The thought of having to attend school on a regular basis does not please me. When we were in school in Graitschen, the school day was often interrupted by air raids. But this is no longer the case. Now, I will have to be in school all day, doing something I would rather avoid as long as possible.

When school starts, the fifth grade is assigned a large room, where each teacher comes to teach his or her subjects. We have about thirty students in a class. Boys and girls are in the same class, unlike the school in Graitschen.

Since we can pick our own seats, I pick a seat in the last row, near the entrance. I feel that if I am some distance from the teacher, I can better avoid being called on to answer questions. It doesn't work. My sister still likes school for some reason. I still don't know why.

My life is boring. I dislike school, and in addition, my father expects me to do my assignments every day after school. Again, he insists on my going over my mathematics assignments with him. He does not realize that, of all the subjects, mathematics is the one I hate most. He tells me that I must do well in mathematics, because someday he hopes that I will work in a bank, just as he did. Again, I do not say anything about this idea.

There is also less food, because some of the food intended for the camp, supposedly, is stolen. Now there are no second servings for soup, and the soup has less meat in it. The only food that is still plentiful is white bread, so I fill my stomach with bread at every meal, and sometimes I put slices of bread in my pocket. Then later at night, when I feel hungry, I eat the bread and feel less hungry.

Besides preparing for school lessons every night and every weekend, my friends and I wander around Wiesbaden on Saturdays and Sundays. This walking seems to make our lives a little more exciting, although, nothing actually happens during this time to make our lives a little more exciting.

The only change is that once a week my parents, my sister, and I, visit a Gasthaus in Wiesbaden. My father seems to have some money, or maybe they use my mother's gold coins to pay for beer and food. We buy sausage and rye bread and vegetable soup. My parents, after much asking, give me a half glass of beer, and when we leave, they have the man behind the counter fill a metal container with beer.

Back in camp, the metal container ends up in our room, and sometimes, when my parents are out of the room, I sip some beer, and this bitter drink fills my stomach and makes me happy.

Time goes by, and it's nearly Christmas. There is no snow, and it is not as cold as in Estonia. Very little happens, and there are no presents to be given. But on Christmas Eve, in the large dining room, everyone is given an orange and a large piece of chocolate wrapped in a dark green piece of paper, which means that the chocolate is from the American army. I don't remember seeing oranges in Estonia, so I feel this one is very special. The chocolate is wonderful and fills my stomach, and the orange is juicy and sweet. It is a good Christmas, after all.

When it comes, I do not see people celebrate the New Year of 1946.

In January, we finish our first half of the school year. I do well in all my subjects—except in mathematics, which is unsatisfactory. When my father sees my report he becomes angry, and tells me I will have to spend much more time preparing my mathematics lessons. I say that I will. What else can I say?

In February and March the weather is warmer, and my friends and I walk to town and to the Rhine River on Saturdays and Sundays. We wander around and look at workers. They are beginning to build houses that were destroyed by the war. I wish we could help instead of sitting in school everyday. When I say this to my friends, they enthusiastically agree.

One spring day, while I am in camp, I am told by my parents that the older brother of one of my schoolmates has drowned in the Rhine River. They say he found a small boat along the riverbank and decided to row across to the other shore. While he was doing this, his small boat got caught in the waves of a barge, and it tipped over. He drowned.

This greatly saddens all of us, because we feel that, now the war has ended, things like this should not happen. But they are still happening, and people are still dying.

A few days after his body is found, we attend a religious gathering in a German building that is used for funerals. His body is burned in the basement. It is a very serious gathering.

We are nearly into summer, 1946. I am twelve years old, my sister is nine years old, and the school year has ended—at last. I improved my mathematics grade slightly, but my father is not happy with it, and he expects me to do better next fall. At least I have the summer ahead.

The Americans in control of the camp are encouraging us to join a new troop of Boy Scouts, and my friends and I join right away. We are all glad to escape our one-room homes. Our parents are all serious and sad because of what happened to them and to their relatives during the war. The Boy Scouts, a teacher says, will give us a chance to sometimes forget the war years. We hope he is right.

Our Scout troop has about twenty members. We are given new uniforms, dark green in color, with a triangular light blue scarf that is tied under the collar with a special knot. Each nationality is given a small patch with its nation's flag stitched on it, and my mother immediately sews mine over my right pocket. She also gives me a new haircut.

We are encouraged to wear the uniform at all times. My friends and I decide to do that, especially since it has been a long time since we have worn something new. This is wonderful.

Joining the Boy Scouts is providing us with much needed daily activities. They include soccer, boxing, and marches in a group to the Rhine River. I enjoy them all, and I am not bored. My friends and I still manage our walks into Wiesbaden, but they are becoming less frequent because of our activities with the Scouts.

As summer moves along, we are given the exciting news that in a few days, Mrs. Roosevelt from America will visit our camp. We are instructed to be ready, and in our Scout uniforms, to welcome her when she arrives. The next week, during a Scout meeting, we suddenly learn that she is coming the next day, and we must gather at noon in the central part of camp.

When she arrives, we are supposed to form a circle around her, hold hands, and as she passes down the street, we are to walk with her and around her. We proudly do as instructed. People line the streets to watch. After walking with her throughout the camp, everyone, including Mrs. Roosevelt, is asked to go to the dining hall where we are served juice and a dark cake. It tastes like chocolate. This is something delicious, which we have not eaten in a long, long time.

Mrs. Roosevelt is very friendly, smiles all the time, and thanks us through an interpreter. Then she leaves the camp in a large green auto. She waves out the open window, and we wave back—feeling very important because we have seen the American president's wife and escorted her throughout our camp.

As early autumn approaches, we are told that some of the refugees from our DP Camp 563 will be moved to another location. We are again worried, because there are always rumors that we may be sent back to our Russian occupied homeland.

However, before long, we receive word that all the Estonians, along with some of the refugees from Latvia and Lithuania, will be sent to Kassel, which is about 150 kilometers to our north. Everyone is relieved, because this means we will be able to remain in Germany under the occupation of the Allies.

While we are awaiting our next move, a small restaurant is opened in camp. It has tables and benches outside, and they mostly serve drinks, such as, juice, beer, and an American drink in a glass bottle. One day, my father takes me and my sister to this place and buys himself a beer, along with two small glass bottles of this dark-colored American drink. The man behind the counter removes the tops of the two bottles, then hands one to me and the other to my sister.

We walk to the table outside, and once seated, I take a swift drink out of my bottle. I immediately begin to choke and cough, and some of the bubbling liquid spurts out of my mouth. I recover fast, and begin to drink small amounts of the liquid. I see that the drink is full of bubbles that seem to explode in my mouth. When I have finished this wonderful, sweet drink, my father tells me that I have just had my first drink of Coca-Cola. My sister, seeing what happened to me, is drinking slowly, without any problems. And she is smiling.

Chapter 40.

EYE INJURY IN WIESBADEN, 1946

One day, at the end of October, some of my friends are gathered outside, and they suggest we play a game of throwing stones at each other. The rule is for one of us to stand behind a tree and another of us to stand behind another tree, a few meters distant. We decide to gather some stones, which we place on the ground behind each tree.

We are allowed to throw a stone at the other person standing behind his tree, and if we hit the tree, we are given one point. The idea is that one of us will throw a stone, and then immediately hide behind his tree, waiting for the other player to throw his stone.

The boy opposite me throws a stone, and as I step from behind my tree to throw my stone, he immediately throws another. Since I no longer have the protection of the tree, his stone hits me hard in my open left eye. I immediately fall to the ground, and my eye explodes with great pain.

I try to stop the pain by rubbing my hurt eye, but that only makes it worse. I try to get up, but I cannot do it, and simply fall back on the ground. Some adults begin to gather around me, and they ask me questions which I cannot understand.

Shortly, a vehicle pulls up to me, and two American soldiers come to me carrying a dark green object like a small bed. They place me on it. One of the soldiers wraps cloth, from a roll, over my eye and the back of my head several times. As they place me on the green object, I feel sick in my stomach, and they place a large towel under my head. They carry my small bed to the green vehicle with a red cross on it, place me inside headfirst, and drive me away.

The pain around my left eye is getting worse. At times, I feel like screaming. After some time, it seems the vehicle is going up a steep hill, because as I lie on the green bed with handles, my head is higher than my feet.

At times, I wonder if I am going to die, and in spite of the pain, I try to think of the story my grandmother told me about the butterfly in spring—if the first butterfly I saw was black, I would die during the year. I try, but I cannot, because of the pain, remember what color butterfly I saw this spring.

I drift in and out of short periods of sleep. The vehicle stops—after what seems forever. The two American soldiers open the back doors and carry me into a building. As soon as we enter, two women in white dresses approach and point toward a room down a hallway. The soldiers carry me to that room, place the bed with handles on the floor, and then lift me onto a bed. They say something to one of the women in white, and leave with the green bed.

As I lie on my back, one of the women begins to remove the bandage that the soldier has put on, then quickly steps back, motioning to the other woman in white to come over.

After the bandage has been removed, I immediately become aware that I cannot see out of my left eye. And I hear one of the women in white say, "Mein Gott!" My God!

The woman then brings over a small mirror and holds it in front of my face. I look into the mirror, and I no longer recognize my own face. The area around my eye is black and dark blue, and the eye itself seems to be gone. "Did it fall out?" I wonder.

As I stare into the mirror, pain returns, and I scream. This pain is far worse than anything I have ever experienced. The women in white help me up, and as I try to stand, my stomach begins to move. They quickly lay me on a bed nearby.

A little while later, I feel a sharp pain in my upper arm, and I am told by one of the women that she has given me an injection for pain. In a short while, the pain has disappeared, and I fall asleep.

I don't know how long I sleep, but I awaken to a man who is wearing a white coat. Once he has my attention, he tells me that he is a German doctor and will decide what to do about my eye. He tells me that I am in the excellent eye hospital in the Taunus Mountains near Wiesbaden. He adds that the two ladies in white are nurses, and they are taking good care of me.

After shining a bright light in my injured eye, he tells me that he has to remove small pieces of sand that have moved behind my eye. He does something, and it feels like my eye has been turned inside out. One of the nurses has handed him a device, and he seems to be spraying water into my eye. After doing this, he again puts a bandage over my injured eye and tells me he will return in two days.

Meanwhile, he says that the nurses, starting tomorrow, will start using a hot patch over my eye, and this should help remove the blood behind my eye. He adds that I will be given medicine for pain, and as he leaves, he tells me that I will not die. This news, in spite of the pain, makes me feel much, much better. The nurses again place me on a bed, and give me a bitter liquid to drink, and I fall asleep.

The doctor returns in a day, and after examining my eye, tells me he now knows my eye is permanently damaged. He tells me that when the rock hit my eye, it was covered by small sand particles. As these became detached, they moved to the back of my eye, and when my eyeball moved, these particles scratched the wall behind my eyeball and left scars.

He says I will be here at least two weeks, during which time the nurses will be placing a heated device on my eye. He also tells the nurses that I can be moved to my own room, in an area with other patients, and I can now walk.

I am walked down a long hall and into a large room with a high ceiling, a bed along the wall, and a table. One nurse takes me to another room and explains that this is where I will eat my meals. The room has a long table in the middle with chairs surrounding it. The nurse tells me that if I feel well enough, I can eat the evening meal tonight, and when the time comes, she will take me to this room. I go back to my room, lie down on the bed, and fall asleep.

I don't know how long I have slept, but I awaken as one of the nurses enters the room. She tells me it is time to eat. As soon as I get up, my eye starts hurting. She tells me I should try to eat, and leads me into the dining room.

As we enter, I see at least ten men seated around the table, and all of them have bandages wrapped around their heads, covering at least one eye. In one case, the man has both eyes covered. The nurse explains to me that these men have all been injured in the war, and some will only get back part of their sight.

One of the men in the group asks me to take a vacant seat next to him, and fills a small metal container with soup from a larger container. He also hands me two slices of rye bread. Some of them begin talking to me, wanting to know what happened to my eye.

As I begin to explain, my eye again begins to hurt, and I try not to show the men I cannot tolerate pain. I eat my soup slowly, look around the table, and realize, even if the war has ended, we are always reminded of war. I can see it at this table.

After I eat the soup and bread, the nurse tells me to come to her room to have my eye covered with a hot pad. She says this will be on for at least two hours, during which time I can return to the dining room or go to my room and sleep. She gives me a spoonful of white powder, which I follow with a glass of water. I again fall asleep in my room, and never get to the dining room.

The following day—much to my surprise and relief—my parents arrive. They were given a ride by an American soldier from the camp. They enter my room, immediately look at my eye, and tell me that I should never throw stones. They tell me they spoke to one of the nurses and were told that I will be seen by a doctor again. However, I will be in the hospital for at least two weeks.

My father tells me they will be moved to another camp. This one is near Kassel, and they will be gone before I am allowed to leave. They also tell me they hope the Americans in the Wiesbaden camp will see to it that I can join them when I am able to leave.

My mother then kisses my cheek, and my father shakes my hand and tells me to be brave. And then, they are gone. After they leave, I sit on my bed for a long time and wonder if I will ever see them again. I know Kassel is 170 kilometers from Wiesbaden.

My thoughts are interrupted by one of the nurses entering my room, followed by two American soldiers. One of them greets me in German and hands me a package wrapped in brown paper. He says they are bringing me food rations. While they stand there, I unwrap the package, and inside I find several metal containers, along with chocolate in dark green wrappings and two small dark green packages.

One of the soldiers tells me the containers are filled with meat and hands me a small pointed metal tool for taking off the top of the container. I immediately recognize this tool, and I tell him I know how to use it. When I take out the small green packages, he tells me these are cigarettes, and since whoever packaged the items did not know my age and sent them along, I can keep these cigarettes.

As they prepare to leave, I thank them, and we shake hands. One of them tells me to get well, and says that they will be back. When they are gone, I put all of the items under my pillow and place the opener device in my pocket.

Before going to the dining room, I decide to take one package of cigarettes along. As we start eating, I take out the pack and offer it to the other patients. They are thankful and quickly divide the cigarettes. As we start eating the soup, they all skim out the small pieces of meat from their soup and place them on my plate.

In a few days, the doctor returns, and after removing the bandage over my eye, he lets me look in a mirror. My eye, and the surrounding area, is still black and blue, and he tells me I must remain in the hospital another ten days. Some of the time passes quickly, because I spend time in the dining room talking with the other patients about the war and their families, and they ask me about my experiences in the war. Treatments for my eye take up lots of time, and I am in bed by eight every night. The two American soldiers come every few days with cigarettes, chocolate, and canned meat. I share the cigarettes and open the cans of meat with the device, and we pass them around, and everyone removes some of the meat and places it in his soup.

But I am getting bored with lying in bed and looking at the high ceiling, and I worry and wonder whether my parents and my sister have moved to Kassel. However, my eye pain is becoming less. The doctor returns and tells me that I have lost most of the sight in my left eye—but I can leave in about three days. I am relieved to hear that I can leave, soon.

He also tells me the nurses will give me a black patch that I will have to wear for several months. As he is leaving, I thank him, and he tells the nurses they should try to make contact with the camp and arrange for my transportation to Kassel. Again, I feel relieved.

A few days later, when I am in my room, one of the nurses enters, followed by two American soldiers. The nurse tells me that today I will be taken by ambulance to Kassel, where the camp has moved. It will take about four hours, and I will again see my family. She also hands me a black patch with strings attached and says I should start wearing it in a few days, after I see another doctor at the Kassel camp.

Before we depart, I go into the dining room where the other patients are gathered, and I walk around and shake their hands and say good-bye. I have two packs of cigarettes in my pocket, and I place them on the dining table. They thank me warmly and wave at me as I leave.

I next enter the nurses' room and say good-bye. I take two cans of meat out of my jacket pockets and give them to one of the nurses to share. She also thanks me warmly, and tells me that I have been very brave, and wishes me well.

The two Americans and I leave the hospital, and one of the soldiers helps me into the back of the army vehicle with red crosses on each side. They have me lie down on a green bed with handles because there are no seats in the back. As we drive away, I look out the small back windows and see the hospital and the Taunus Mountains fade into the background.

The slow drive takes what seems forever, and I am beginning to think about my future. I hope the eye injury will keep me out of school. Finally, the ambulance stops. The American soldiers open the rear door and walk me into a building that looks like a hospital, because I see women in white coats.

One of the soldiers hands a large envelope to one of the nurses. While pointing at me, he tells her something. As they turn to leave, they come over, and we shake hands. I thank them for the trip, and they leave. I turn around once more to look at them leaving, and as I do, I see writing in large letters on the back of the ambulance saying, "Spaghetti Wagon." I think that must be how you say ambulance in English.

A nurse tells me to sit down, and she removes the bandage. When it is off, she makes a strange sound and calls over another nurse. They quickly lead me to a bed, make me lie down, and tell me that they will try to locate my parents.

She asks me if my eye hurts and I tell her it does. She immediately places a white powder in a glass, fills it with water, and hands it to me. I drink it, and a few moments later the pain is gone, and I become drowsy.

In a few hours, my parents arrive. They seem to be angry and again tell me not to throw rocks. Although I have heard this before, I nod my head and quickly agree not to throw—anything.

One of the nurses tells them that I can go tonight, but I must return once a day for at least two weeks. Every day, the nurse will cover my eye with a heat patch, so the blood behind my injured eye will disappear.

I am thankful to be with my family again.

Chapter 41.

ANOTHER HOME, THIS TIME IN KASSEL

Our new home is in a two-story building occupied by four families. We share the gas stove in the kitchen, and every family has its own room. We no longer eat in a dining hall, but are given rations from the Americans, like those I was given in the hospital—plus potatoes, bread, oatmeal, and flour. Although we have very little meat, we now have less of a shortage of food. This camp is unlike the earlier ones, because it is not fenced in—and that is good. It is at the edge of town, which will make it easy to walk to the bomb-damaged town. It seems a little smaller than Wiesbaden, and I hope they have a Boy Scout troop in this camp.

School has started, and I am assigned to the sixth grade. We still have the Estonian teachers, and boys and girls are taught together. I no longer see as much of my sister because she has girlfriends her age. She still likes school. I cannot imagine why.

Unfortunately, I am not excused from school because of my eye injury. I go to school in the morning. Then, I am happy to be excused in the afternoon to go to the camp's medical clinic, where the nurses apply the heated patch to my injured eye.

When I am not in the clinic I am required to wear the black eye patch. Many of the students laugh at me because of the patch, but my closest friends do not. I personally enjoy the patch, because I think it makes me look older. To add to this older look, I try to make lines in my face by squinting my good eye, and when I am alone, pushing my cheeks together with my hands to make creases. I see the boy who hit me with the rock, and he is still a good friend.

I also get by with less schoolwork, because I tell my teachers and parents that with the pain in my eye, I have trouble reading. Everyone seems to understand, and after a while, the students no longer make fun of the black patch. After a few weeks, I am no longer required to go to the medical clinic.

But I miss those visits because now, again, I am required to attend school all day. The area around my eye is no longer black and blue, but I still wear the black patch. Although the pain is mostly gone, I like to complain that it has not left, because I am, then, allowed to leave school.

Christmas arrives, and it is, again, a sad time. We gather in our room on Christmas Eve and talk about our relatives left behind, not knowing what has happened to them. My mother begins crying, and my sister joins in, followed by my father and me. My friends tell me they have the same sad celebrations with their families.

Early in 1947, I am told that I no longer need to wear the eye patch. Others no longer laugh at me, but I miss wearing the patch, because I could use it as an excuse for getting a headache and being sent home. I am sure I also looked older with it on.

Time in Kassel passes and spring arrives. I become thirteen years old, and my sister becomes ten. People tell me I am tall for my age, and I hope this makes me look older.

Luckily, there is a Boy Scout troop, and I like it because it gives me and my friends something to do, and because sometimes we are given extra food at meetings. When school ends, our troop begins hiking, and whenever the sun is out, we go swimming in a pool outside the city.

One day, at the pool, we sit on the side watching a man dive off the board. During one of his dives, he spins around, and the back of his head hits the board. When he lands in the water, he does not begin to swim. He lies still and then he begins to sink.

We run to the small building at the end of the pool and, hastily, tell the man in charge of the pool what has happened. We see that this man has only one good leg—the other has been amputated below the knee. He follows us, half-running, on his crutches. As we point out where the diver is, he quickly removes his trousers and shirt and dives in.

A short while later, he surfaces, cradling the diver's head and supporting him with one arm across his chest. By now, a small crowd has gathered, and some of the adults quickly jump into the pool and help lift the diver onto the edge.

As the man is lifted from the pool, I look at his face and see wide-open eyes that seem to look at me. There is no life in those eyes, and I am reminded, once more, of death—which I have seen or heard about so often in these past years.

My thoughts are interrupted by the arrival of an ambulance and two American soldiers, who begin to push on the man's chest as he lies on his back with his eyes wide open. After a while, the soldiers place his lifeless body in the ambulance and drive off. My friends and I decide to return to the camp. We no longer feel like swimming. In fact, I do not know how to swim, and I wonder if I want to learn. I know I never want to dive.

As summer comes to an end, we are notified that the camp will, again, be moved. This time our new destination will be Geislingen an Steige, which is about four hundred kilometers southeast of our present location. We are told that we should be ready to leave with a day's notice.

It seems to me that whenever I become accustomed to a new home, we have to move again. This is when my thoughts return to the Tuule Farm, and I wonder how my grandparents are. I miss them. I wonder if my future will always involve moving. But at the same time, I find my life exciting because of all the changes—and with fewer school days.

One day, we are told by the camp's administration that we are expected to go to the nearest railroad station the following morning, with all of our belongings. Early the next day, we carry our two suitcases, the small red suitcase, and my backpack, to the station where the train with freight cars is waiting. My father carries his own briefcase, which he never loses.

Two American soldiers instruct the crowd of several hundred that we will be assigned approximately twenty-five people to each car. The train will be leaving in a few hours, and our destination is Geislingen an der Steige, southeast of Stuttgart, on the way to Augsburg and Munich.

We are informed that we will be given food rations shortly, and we should stay close to our assigned freight car. When we receive the rations, I open my package and discover a package of cigarettes. I remove the cigarettes and tuck them into my pocket, making sure that no adults have seen them. I know, at some time, I can trade them for food, as I did at the eye hospital.

A short time later, the locomotive blows its whistle, and we are ordered to get into our assigned freight car. We do as we are told, and without any further warning, the train begins to move. I decide to eat my rations, opening the tin can of meat with the small can opener I always keep in my pocket. Then I cut the meat with my pocketknife. I always enjoy the taste of this canned meat.

The train moves very slowly, and I choose to sit in the open freight car door, watching Kassel pass by and, eventually, disappear from sight.

As the train begins to pick up speed, the passengers settle down, finding seats on their bags and suitcases. I continue to sit in the open doorway with my legs hanging out. When my mother sees me, she promptly orders me to get inside. I do as I am told, because I know there is no point in telling her that I am fine in the doorway. I find my backpack and decide to simply lie down and, hopefully, fall asleep. This is exactly what happens.

When I awake, the train has stopped. It is dark outside. Everyone has left the train car. I look at the spot where some men had been playing cards, and notice a half-full bottle of wine.

I quickly look around to see if someone is watching, but no one is there. So I pick up the bottle and drink out of it. I take another drink and replace the bottle. I sense a warm feeling in my mouth and throat, and take another drink, being careful to leave some wine in the bottle. It reminds me of the days in Graitschen, when the kindly bartender gave me a half glass of beer.

As I get out of the train, I see my parents and sister nearby. I join them and ask my father why we have stopped. He tells me that since we are traveling in freight cars, and there are no toilets, the train has to stop about every hour and let people go to the toilets at stations.

As he finishes his explanation, the locomotive whistle blows, and again we all board our assigned freight car. I enter the boxcar, locate my spot, lie down, and fall asleep.

The next thing I know, the train is stopped in a freight yard. As I get up, I hear a conversation saying that we have finally arrived in Geislingen.

Chapter 42.

GEISLINGEN AN DER STEIGE

The town is located approximately fifty kilometers southeast of Stuttgart. We are all ordered to exit the box cars, with our bags, and wait for instructions. In a short while, army trucks begin to arrive. We are instructed to gather in family groups and wait for our names to be called, at which time we are to get on a truck.

In no time, our family and four others, are told to get on a certain truck, and once we are on, the vehicle starts off toward our unknown destination. After driving through the city, the truck stops in front of a two-story, light-colored stucco house, which looks like a private home. We are instructed to enter the home and wait for an assignment to a particular room. We are assigned to a large room equipped with bunk beds, a table, and four chairs. As my parents discuss who will sleep where, I leave the room and begin to explore our new home.

It is different from anything we have occupied since leaving Estonia in August, 1944. The house is beautiful, with a red-tiled roof. It is very clean, and has a large kitchen which will be shared by the four other families who will live here with us. When I walk outside, I enter a large fenced garden which has a railroad track behind it. I feel lucky to finally be at a destination that seems permanent. But I wonder which German family we have replaced. I feel bad about putting them out of their home.

The house is located on Rappenackern Street. However, I learn that our actual address is International Refugee Organization (IRO), Camp 615 172-8, Geislingen an der Steige. The last part of the address means that the city of Geislingen is located on the Steige River.

When I return to the house, my parents tell me we must go to a building nearby to be given food rations. I decide to stay behind, and explore, when my parents and sister leave. They return in an hour carrying two bags of food which contain two loaves of rye bread, several cans of American army food, canned meat, oatmeal, small bags of powdered milk, and some potatoes. Because we can only get food once a week, it seems that this is not enough. My mother is in charge of the food and divides it into daily rations. She will make it last.

After I get used to our new home, I become bored. Very little is exciting, and I begin to explore the countryside with my friends from Kassel. We discover the ruins of an old castle not far from town, and this adds a little adventure as we explore it. However, it does not have a buried virgin in it, nor a glowing light at night like our backyard castle in Viljandi.

During this time, my father begins to work in the camp administration building as an interpreter, because he can speak German and some English. He is paid a small amount for this, which can be used to purchase additional food, mainly bread, because this is sometimes all the stores in town have to sell. He says he enjoys working with the American soldiers, and the work gives him a chance to improve his speaking of the English language.

As we approach August, 1947, we learn, through our parents, that anyone twelve or older, can go to a YMCA camp nearby, on top of a small mountain called Kuhberg. The camp will begin in mid-August and last for two weeks. My friends and I all look forward to camp, hoping it will add some excitement to our lives.

It occurs to me, that every time our family moves, everybody moves, so we keep our old friends and schoolmates, and everybody knows one another. If we were home in Estonia, we would probably all have jobs, and we would not be wandering around looking for something to do. At the very least, I would have a job herding sheep and cattle on the Tuule Farm every summer.

Meanwhile, as we await the YMCA camp, we are organized into a Boy Scout troop, and the Scout leader takes us on marches to neighboring villages. He tells us that we have to be ready for the camp in August. We agree with him and are willing to march anywhere he suggests.

When camp time arrives, we are told to gather on a certain day, and take along a change of clothing. Luckily, we have received some clothes from America. I have been given some canvas shoes, with high tops and laces, from the American army. They are the green color the army uses. Now I feel ready for camp. We are taken there on several army trucks, about thirty to a truck. I think there are about one hundred campers, plus some adults to direct us.

When we arrive, we are assigned to large army tents with twelve of us assigned to each tent. These are equipped with collapsible canvas army beds, and we are given a pillow and two dark green army blankets. An adult is assigned to each tent, which is a good thing.

We are told about the daily activities which will consist of group hikes and sports activities, such as, soccer and running races. We are assigned to teams for the soccer games that will take place every day. We can also expect to play our plastic flutes, given to us by our Scout troop in Wiesbaden. These we will play in small groups. Fortunately, I am good at playing this flute. We are told that we have to go to bed by 9:00 p.m. and rise at 6:00 a.m., and we are instructed to bathe under the outdoor water faucets, and to brush our teeth after meals.

Breakfast is oatmeal and two slices of rye bread. Lunch is thin soup and rye bread, and our evening meal is army food that comes in tin cans. There seems to be enough food, and I am certain we will not feel the hunger we have experienced in the past. This is good.

After a few days, we begin the sports. Soccer seems to be the most popular, and I am chosen as one of the defenders. Of course, I am chosen last, because I am not very good. I only learned the game in Wiesbaden, but I am willing to play. We begin play, and about halfway into the first game, while I am defending the goal from an attacker, I am kicked in my right ankle, and I drop down in pain. The coach approaches me and tells me to get up and play, but when I get up and step hard on my right foot, I feel extreme pain. He orders me to leave the field and sit down and replaces me with another player. Actually, I think he is happy to be rid of me.

As I sit on a bench, the pain becomes worse. Eventually, one of the adults tells me to go to the camp nurse. After a painful walk, dragging my injured foot and ankle, I arrive at the nurse's tent. She gives me a short examination and tells me that I have a bad sprain.

She wraps the ankle tightly in a heavy bandage and tells me to go to my tent and lie down. She adds, I should not participate in any sports activities. She gives me a white pill to swallow, and instructs me to come and see her the following day.

I decide to like my new situation of having a sprained ankle and not having to compete in sports. I can spend the day watching others participate. Now my life is simpler without having to do well on a soccer field. I see the nurse daily, and show up for three meals a day, and I am happy.

When Sunday arrives, my parents, along with my sister, visit the camp. My sister tells me that she misses me and that she would like to stay in the camp. This is not possible, because she is too young. I remind her that she is busy with the ballet lessons that she is so good at. However, if there is another camp the following year, she can go. My parents tell me that they will not be able to visit again because it is a long walk, which takes them about two hours each way. I understand.

Every day is the same. But I do enjoy the leisure of not having to participate in sports. I continue to like the daily visits to the nurse, who gives me a pill that seems to eliminate the pain in my ankle.

As time goes on, there are more boys who become injured. The number of participants in sports is decreasing. All we have to do is sit on the sidelines and watch others work. It is very enjoyable. Before I know it, the camp is coming to an end, and when we return to Geislingen, the time for school is fast approaching.

One fine day, we are ordered to report for school. The school is an old building with classrooms and noisy stairs. I am assigned to the seventh school year, and at age thirteen, I am not certain if I am behind in my placement. In any event, I am assigned the following classes: Religion,

Estonian, English, German, History, Algebra, Geometry, Natural Science, Physics, Geography, Drawing and History of Art, Gymnastics, Manual Instruction, and Singing. Some of them worry me, especially, those having to do with mathematics. We will also be evaluated for the following forms of behavior: Conduct, Diligence, and Orderliness.

The first day of school, we are assigned a permanent classroom, and we are allowed to pick our own seats. The rows of seats are elevated, like those in a Roman arena, so even if I choose the last row, which I prefer, I cannot hide from the teacher. However, I still choose the last row, hoping that I will be less visible.

I know most of the teachers who taught in the other camps, and I get along with all of them. We still stand when a teacher enters the room, and we, also, rise when we are called upon to answer a question. No one ever misbehaves.

Since school has started, my days really have become very boring. In the evening, after I have spent a day in school, my father asks me about my homework and assignments. He insists on spending at least an hour every evening doing algebra and geometry. These must have been his favorites. Now I have to do my lessons in his presence, and he continues to get upset when I make mistakes. Which I often do.

My sister, three years younger, is only two years behind me in school and is very eager to do her homework. She is a much better student and, actually, likes school and homework. I can't help but think of the wartime, which is over two years in the past. Although I didn't like the war, it had certain benefits, as far as I am concerned. When the air raid sirens sounded we were sent home, which shortened the school days, considerably, and as the end of war drew closer and the air raids became more frequent, I could not help but welcome them.

As time goes on, my life becomes very ordinary. One day is much like any other, and I wish that I could forget school and do something else, like the work I did at the Tuule Farm. But this, I know, is out of the question.

Because my ankle is still painful, I am at least excused from athletic events. However, I miss the weekend hikes I would be taking with the Boy Scouts. On Sundays, some of my friends and I explore the town of Geislingen. We discover a Gasthaus where we can enter through the rear, and the bartender gives us small glasses of beer. I pay for these with money my father has given me—although, I do not tell him for what I am spending it. This beer makes me feel better and less bored.

We go through a food line for rations once a week. Much of the food is army rations, and they are very tasty. We could easily eat everything in about four days, but all the items have to be separated and divided by my mother to last for seven days. There is plenty of oatmeal, and often we eat it twice a day.

There are still times when I go to bed hungry, and if my parents have some beer in their metal container, which they have had since living in Graitschen in the fall of 1944, I drink some of it without their knowledge. Then, I do not feel the hunger. I am growing. Some say I am tall for thirteen years of age.

One day, when we stand in line for food, I observe a man in front of us. When he is given an item that is not packaged, like bread, butter, or a slice of sausage, he eats it right away. The people distributing the food become angry, and he is led away from the food line. Someone says he is trying to show that there is not enough food for the week. I wonder what he will eat for the rest of the week, since he has eaten much of his food while going through the line.

I am finally getting used to school. I realize that there is no way I can avoid it, and I manage to do the assignments. My father seems, somewhat, satisfied.

Time passes. Every Sunday, my parents ask me to take my sister for a walk, and we go through town. There is nothing to do, other than look at old buildings and the many other walkers. We walk, and we look. Then we look, and we walk.

Eventually, Christmas arrives. Christmas Eve, we stay home. There is no tree. It is a sad time, because always my parents think of their parents and all those left behind, and they are very worried about them. My mother says that if they are alive, they are probably also thinking of us, and wondering if we are alive.

As she talks about them, she begins to cry, and before I know it, my sister is crying. My father seems to avoid the tears, but I cannot manage to do so. Surprisingly, there are mittens for me and my sister and a scarf for my father. My mother somehow managed to knit these items without us knowing. We are grateful for our presents, and I walk to my mother and give her a hug and tell her that I am sorry because I have no present for her, and she tells me that a hug is better than a present. Next year, I promise myself, I will do better.

My father, with a smile on his face, takes a bottle of perfume out of his pocket for my mother, and he brings out a bottle of wine from somewhere. He pours a glassful for my mother and himself, and then pours a small amount into glasses for me and my sister. He holds his glass up in the air, and we all click the glasses together and wish each other, "Merry Christmas."

I drink mine very slowly. As my sister drinks hers, a disappointed look appears on her face. She obviously doesn't like the taste, and I ask her to pour it into my glass. I then walk to my bed and take out half a bar of dark army chocolate and hand it to her, and she gives me a kiss on my cheek. I give her a hug, and she immediately begins to eat the chocolate, as I drink my wine very slowly, hoping to have it last, forever. Before long, the Christmas Eve has passed, and we all go to bed.

New Year's Eve arrives, and my parents invite some friends to celebrate. They drink wine, and our room is filled with laughter, rather then with the tears which marked Christmas Eve. My sister and I meet some of my friends who live in our building. We play dominos in the shared kitchen. One of my friends has a partially filled bottle of wine that he found in his room. We pass it around from one to another, but my sister refuses to have a drink. The bottle seems to empty fast. My friend takes the empty bottle outside and hides it under some bushes. We all seem very happy, and before long, the evening has reached midnight and the New Year, 1948, is here. The adult guests are leaving, and some appear to have trouble walking. My sister and I return to our room, and everyone goes to sleep.

Sometime, during January, rumors begin to circulate among the adults, that the occupying armies of America, England, and France have been ordered by Russia to leave Berlin. This means if Russians were to attack the other forces, it would lead to war with Russia, and many believe our homeland would then be liberated, and we could all go home.

But it soon becomes clear that the Russians will not attack the other forces, and the possibility of our return becomes very unlikely. Once more, people are disappointed.

School passes, and I am now into the second phase of grade seven. I somehow manage to get by. I receive one academic grade of Excellent, which is in Religion, and I also do well in English, History, Natural Sciences, Geography, Gymnastics, and Singing. What's remarkable is the fact that I do well in Conduct, Diligence, and Orderliness. Although these last three areas are not academic, they put me into a category of students who have no behavioral problems, and therefore, are not under the watchful eyes of the teachers. It's simply a situation of being left alone by the teachers, if one behaves.

The academic areas of Algebra and Geometry leave a lot to be desired. Since I do not do well—and I am already getting pressure from my father—I expect long evenings of working on these two subjects.

There is very little in my life that is exciting, and time drags by very slowly. My parents do allow me to stay in the Boy Scouts, and this, at least, gets me out of our crowded room. My friends feel as I do.

In early spring, rumors begin to circulate about the refugees from Russian controlled countries having the opportunity to emigrate to other countries in western Europe, and possibly, to Australia, Canada, and even, America.

My father has obtained a French passport, and he is considering the possibility of visiting France and exploring job opportunities there. He feels that with his banking background, he can probably find something, even if his French language is limited. Although he talks about it, the visit never materializes. Instead, as time goes on, he feels that it would be wiser to wait for Australia, Canada, or America to offer us the opportunity to emigrate.

My parents decide to make application for all of them, and my father fills out the necessary papers. We have our pictures taken at a local photo shop, and my father sends these along with the applications. Now we can only wait and hope.

Meanwhile, the overwhelming hope, for everyone, is the possibility that our homeland will somehow be liberated from the Russian occupation, and we will all be able to return home. People always hope.

When June arrives, the Russians shut off train and highway travel to Berlin. All supplies coming from the West to Berlin must now be flown in by the Allies. We are at least five hundred kilometers away from Berlin, so we are not worried about our safety, but rumors immediately circulate about the Western Allies simply using their armed forces to forge their way to Berlin. If war becomes a reality, we think our homeland will be liberated from Russian occupation. Nothing of this nature, however, takes place, and our attention is again drawn to emigration.

In the meantime, my spring semester in school has ended, and I have been elevated to the eighth grade. Although my overall academic performance is satisfactory, I again do poorly in my father's mind. Unexpectedly, my best grade of Excellent is, once more, in Religion. Quite frankly, my father does not seem to care about my poor performance in Algebra and Geometry, and I think that he has given up the hope that, someday, I will follow in his footsteps. I am very relieved that, hopefully, I will no longer be subjected to after school mathematics sessions under his watchful eye. Truthfully, I think his attention is on the matter of emigration.

In early summer, my father, with two friends from Estonia who also live in the camp, decides to visit southern Germany by train. Surprisingly, I am invited to go along, and I am very eager about it, because this is the first time, since the end of war, that I will be staying somewhere other than in a new camp. What an adventure. I tell my friends about the trip, and I can see they think I am really lucky and wish they could, somehow, go along.

Before we leave, my father tells me that he is paying for the trip by selling some of the gold coins that my mother has brought from Estonia. I think he is selling them on the black market, because where else would you sell them? I know most things are traded on the black market these days. There is very little for sale in the stores.

Our vacation destination is the Garmisch-Partenkirchen area near the Austrian border, approximately two-hundred kilometers away. We plan to be gone for about an entire week, and we take the train to get there. It is wonderful, because we do not travel in the boxcars, but in the regular passenger cars.

When we arrive, I am thrilled to see the German Alps, which I had never thought I would see. The trip also pleases me, because this is the first time that I am spending any time with my father, and away from a camp, since the end of war. I find my father and I are good friends when we do not have mathematics to discuss.

While we are here, we stay in the attic of a private home and eat our meals in a different Gasthaus every day. We eat mainly sausage and rye bread, and it all tastes wonderful. Among other excursions, we visit a nearby salt mine. We board an open small train and when we are inside the salt mine, I am reminded of air raid shelters that we were in during the war, because it is underground. But this is a new experience, and I like traveling on this little car with wheels and walls so near. And without sirens and bombs.

However, the most exciting part of this trip is the visit to Zugspitze, which is the highest Alpine mountain in Germany. To reach the top of the mountain, we ride on a train which is built to reach high points by the use of a third rail in the middle of the two regular rails. To add to the excitement, the track runs close to a steep drop-off on one side. The weather is warm, and the sun is shining. What an adventure.

On top, we get off the train, and the view is thrilling, because there is nothing in sight except the mountains and the sky. There are no trees growing this high. There are no bombed buildings or fences or barracks or people. None of us has ever visited a mountain before, because Estonia is flat, except for small hills, and we all agree that this is amazing. After wandering around on the rocks in the fresh air for a few hours, we must, reluctantly, return on the train with three rails to the Garmisch-Partenkirchen area.

The next day, we return to Geislingen and we hurry to tell my mother and my sister all about our adventure. When I meet my friends, I also tell them about the trip, and I can see that they all wish they could have gone along. Someday, we say, we will travel everywhere together.

The summer continues less dramatically, and as July arrives, we again receive word of the YMCA camp on Kuhberg Mountain, where I spent time the previous summer. Unfortunately, my ankle has healed and I will most likely be expected to participate in sports.

This time, I am told, my sister will also be going to camp, and my parents tell me to take care of her. I am now fourteen years old and my sister is eleven. Much to my delight, she is very happy to go to camp, and I hope that, since I am expected to be her guardian, I will be able to avoid sports.

When camp starts, we are again living in army tents, and the meals are sufficient and I do not feel any hunger. My sister's camp is a short walk from ours, and every night before bedtime, I walk to her tent and kiss her goodnight. I have saved some army candy bars, and every night I give her a piece of chocolate, so she won't get homesick. I also talk with the sports people and tell them that, as her guardian, I will be unable to find the time to be on any teams. They accept this. I am set at ease.

One weekend, our parents visit and bring along a postcard addressed to me from my godmother Hilda, who is now living in England. The postcard has on it four British postage stamps announcing the Olympic Games which are taking place in England this year. I consider this a special treat and decide to make this card, and its stamps, a part of my stamp collection that I started after the end of the war. I have been exchanging stamps with my friends, and I have two albums that are nearly full. I have heard that rare stamps, especially from the Nazi era, will someday be valuable, and I think, someday, I will have lots of money when I decide to sell my collection. I guard my two albums. They are usually hidden under my mattress, no matter which camp we are in.

Our stay at the camp goes along well, and I am spending time with my sister, making sure that she enjoys her new experience of being away from our parents and not missing them. When she is not in any activities for the girls, I take her to watch soccer games and running races and make sure she sits at my table for breakfast, lunch, and dinner. She does not get homesick.

When the camp ends, and we return home, it is only a short time before school begins. I feel a certain amount of boredom returning to me even before we start school. But the day comes, and I begin the eighth grade. The subjects I am taking are mostly the same, except Chemistry has been added to my class schedule.

During my free time in the fall, I do enjoy the Boy Scout activity of taking ten-to-fifteen mile hikes and camping out overnight. We like to explore the countryside surrounding Geislingen. Once, when we are marching through a nearby village, several children who are angry and have eyes which seem to come out of the sides of their faces, not straight ahead like our eyes, throw stones at us and run after us. We do not fight with them, but continue marching very fast, as our Scout leader commands. They really are different looking children, however, and I wonder why there are so many of them in one village.

Some of my friends enjoy climbing steep cliffs on a nearby hill. As they descend from the top, often helped by someone holding a rope, they discover small caves cut into the side of the cliff. Because I am fearful of any heights, I usually manage to produce an excuse for why I am unable to take part in these cliff climbing adventures. I do not want to show cowardice, so there are even times that I become involved in a sport activity, such as volleyball, just to have a good excuse for not wanting to climb on a cliff. Sometimes, my life becomes disordered as I try to avoid certain activities.

However, I do enjoy tying the knots that our Scout leader teaches us. He seems pleased with my efforts, and this makes up, somewhat, for my lack of skill in sports. I hope.

Chapter 43.

IMMIGRATION PLANS

In October, my parents tell me they are going to contact the National Lutheran Council in New York. Apparently, they have given up on any chance countries occupied by the Soviets will become free again. They feel if an opportunity comes for us to go to the United States, they will certainly take advantage of it.

On November 23, my father receives a telegram from Wingate Lucas of the House of Representatives in Washington D.C., USA, who resides in Fort Worth, Texas USA, telling my father that our application for entry into the United States has been forwarded to Alf and Jessie Cozby, who own a Barbeque Restaurant in Fort Worth, Texas. The telegram also states that the Cozbys are in a position to sponsor us as immigrants to the United States. I think this means they can give us work and a place to live.

My parents are distraught by the realization that if we go to the United States, the chance of our return to Estonia will never happen, and we will never see our relatives again. I feel the same fear. But, some days, we feel it is best for us to go. Our feelings go back and forth, and back and forth. It is a very emotional time.

I have lost all interest in school, and all I do is think about leaving Germany. It would be nice to have a real home. I try to do reasonably well in my English class, however, because I would like to be able to have some ability to speak the language when we arrive in America. My parents have an Estonian-English dictionary, and we all use it. Often.

In the meantime, food is still in short supply, and one day my mother takes a train to a nearby farming village, not far from Geislingen, in hope of buying some food. She visits a farm, but the only item she can take back, hidden from view, is butter.

She buys two packages of butter wrapped in pieces of cloth. She attaches the two pieces inside her coat, one at each shoulder, with safety pins, so they cannot be seen by anyone, because the buying of food, unless purchased in a store, is considered buying from the black market—and is illegal. We know all the items purchased outside of a store can be taken away, and the buyer can get in trouble.

My mother is very careful as she rides home on the train with her large shoulders, and we are very pleased to taste the good butter on our oatmeal or in the potato and onion sandwiches she prepares for us.

My mother also takes walks into the country and exchanges some of her remaining gold Russian coins for other food items. One day, she returns with a live duck she expects my father to kill. She plans to roast it for supper.

When my sister sees the duck, she immediately likes it—and she adopts it as a pet. It becomes clear that she will be very sad if her pet is killed, and my parents decide not to kill it. Instead, my father clips the ends of the duck's wings and builds a small enclosure in which the duck is kept, and admired, by my sister. Rather than becoming food for the family, the duck is, actually, eating part of our daily food supply.

In the middle of December, my parents receive a letter from a Lutheran minister, Earl Moehring, of Jourdanton, Texas, which was sent on December 5. This letter welcomes us to Texas, whenever that happens. We also receive a letter from the Cozbys, and it describes a 112 acre farm and a house we will be living in. We will be expected to operate the farm, of which thirty-five acres are tillable. I am looking forward to this, because I hope it will be like my grandparents' farm.

My parents are finally relieved that we will find a new home where there is no war, even though it remains very hard to think of living so far away from Estonia. We all shed happy, and sad, tears. Often.

We are again approaching Christmas, and as before, it is not a happy time. When Christmas Eve arrives, we sit in our room, and my mother begins to cry as she talks about our relatives who were left behind. She talks about our going to America, and the fact we will never see our relatives again. Once again, we are all crying and hugging.

Again, I am glad when Christmas passes and New Year's Eve arrives. The adults gather and drink wine and beer, and the mood is happier. There is always some beer and wine left in glasses or bottles for me to sneak out of the room and share with my friends. I am convinced that beer and wine are here to make us happy.

It is now 1949. In the middle of January, my parents receive a letter from the Cozbys in which Mr. Cozby makes reference to awaiting notice of our arrival in New York. This is news to us, because we have not heard officially of our acceptance as immigrants. But shortly, we are notified by the Camp Administration that we will probably be leaving for America in the middle of February. We consider that we must now be officially accepted, and because of this, we feel free to move on with plans for leaving Germany.

One day, our family is called to go to the camp clinic. We must have chest X-rays taken, along with some other procedures, to assure that we are free of disease. After the exams have been done, we are told that my sister and I each have a spot on our lungs, which means that we have a history of tuberculosis. Her condition is considered cured, but I have to return for further tests.

I am very concerned, because if I have TB, I will be left behind when my parents and sister leave. I would be put in a hospital again. I would much rather travel with my family. After waiting a few days, my parents are told that my tuberculosis is also cured. My worries are over. We are now able to go to America together. What a relief!

All we are doing is waiting as to the time of departure, and at the end of January, we are told that we will certainly depart during the second week of February. Although I am in school every day, I have no interest in it. I am living in anticipation of our departure. We all are.

Because we will be crossing the Atlantic Ocean on a ship, I cannot avoid thinking about the Baltic crossing in August, 1944, when we were attacked by Russian planes and a Russian submarine. My thoughts return to that escape and what would have happened had the torpedo hit the ship—or a bomb from a plane hit us. I try not to think of it.

Some of my fellow students are also scheduled to leave, either for Canada or America. All we do is talk about our forthcoming journeys. We are all ready to leave for new adventures. This time without war. We promise to keep up with one another through letters.

One day, at the end of January, my parents receive a telegram saying we depart from Hamburg sometime in the second week of February. In early February, I receive my eighth grade mid-year report card, indicating I no longer have to attend school in Geislingen. The report contains my final grades. Most of my grades are satisfactory, but amazingly, again, my Excellent grade is in Religion. This, of course, somewhat upsets my father, because he had still hoped for an Excellent in mathematics. I had hoped that he would be too busy with our preparations for departure to notice my grades. But this is not the case.

Fortunately, his attention is diverted when he receives a letter from the National Lutheran Council in New York City, telling us to meet Mr. Cozby at a New York City hotel upon our arrival. We will be notified as to the date, and once there, we will be driven by Mr. Cozby to Fort Worth, Texas. My father has a map of the United States, and it looks like a very long drive. Much longer than a drive all across Estonia.

Before long, we are given a departure date, February 7, for leaving the camp on an army truck. It will drive us to the train in Geislingen. We are told that after we are placed on the train, we will be taken to the harbor of Bremerhaven. The excitement is building with each new directive we are given.

On February 6, the night before we leave, my parents have a gathering in our room, and friends stop in to say good-bye. As usual, there is beer and wine. There is, also, a lot of hugging—but no tears. Some of the

Estonians sign my mother's visitor book, which is an Estonian custom. Among those signing is Johann Holberg, our former Minister of War in Estonia. Since the room is full, I am able to drink small amounts of wine and beer. This makes me happy, and I no longer worry about the trip being like the Moltkefels crossing of August, 1944.

The following morning, we sit on our two suitcases with my mother's small red case and my backpack and my father's briefcase, in front of our latest home on Rappenackern Street, in Geislingen an Steige. An army truck pulls up and stops. We climb on board and find a place to sit among the other passengers. As the truck pulls away, we exchange hand waves with our friends left behind, among them my friend, Rjurik, who has volunteered to take our duck and care for it.

Shortly, we arrive at the railroad station, and after a wait of about an hour, board the arriving passenger train. I note that this is the first time, since Estonia, we have not had to travel in boxcars as a family. We easily find seats and stuff our belongings under them.

I have checked my father's map prior to our leaving, and I think our destination is approximately 550 kilometers north of Geislingen. I ask a train conductor for the exact distance. He tells me that it is about the same as my calculation. As the train begins to leave, I think about our departures since Estonia, and there have been many from August of 1944 to now. This is the most momentous.

The train frequently stops along the way, and not always in stations. We finally arrive in Bremerhaven, northern Germany, the next day. We are immediately taken by an army truck to temporary housing, which looks like German navy barracks, because Bremerhaven is on the North Sea.

We, again, share large rooms and are fed in a dining hall with other refugees. We are told we will be here at least another week because other displaced persons will be arriving from different locations. As soon as there are enough passengers to fill the ship, we will be departing for America. Someone in the barracks tells us the ship's capacity is approximately 3,800 passengers. People keep arriving from several DP camps throughout the western part of Germany, and during the last part of the second week, it looks like we will really be leaving. We are ready.

The very next morning, we are driven to the harbor on another army truck and unloaded next to a large, grey American troop ship. I see that the ship's name is Marine Tiger.

We, and the others, immediately walk up a gangplank with our possessions. This time, my sister does not have to be led by her hand. She carries her own bag. On the deck, our papers are inspected by an American naval officer. The ship quickly becomes noisy and busy and buzzing with excitement.

Now the language is all in English. I am thankful that I have studied English in school for four years. I can understand what people are saying to us. My sister understands, also, and we interpret what our parents do not understand.

Men and boys are given separate quarters from women and girls. My mother and sister go to locate their quarters, and my father and I hurry to locate bunks in the men's quarters. We are assigned bunk beds that are four beds high, the tallest I have ever seen, and they are located within large rooms housing about sixty people.

My father gets a bottom bunk for himself, and I settle on one directly above him. There are electric lights, because we are below the level of the portholes that provide natural light. We are told the lights will remain on day and night, in contrast to the dim war conditions we had on the blacked-out Moltkefels. We place our belongings on the bunks, which will be our beds for approximately ten days, and return on deck.

Later that morning, as we all stand on deck, the ship begins to blow its shrill whistles, the boarding ramp leading to the ship is taken away, and I see men removing heavy chains that have held the ship to the dock. Finally, the ship begins to move, pulled by tugboats, and we solemnly look toward land, and say good-bye to Germany, which has saved us from the Russians for nearly five years.

As the piercing whistles continue to blow, there is expectation and exhilaration amongst the passengers. As we pull out, only sea gulls follow us, instead of bombers. No one is wearing a double layer of clothes. There is no one-legged accordion player, nor are there starving Russian prisoners, nor wounded horses, nor crying babies—and we have been reunited as a family. We feel very fortunate and hopeful. I will be fifteen years old next month, and my sister will be twelve years old. My father is forty-four, and my mother will be forty-one in April. We are all in good health and excellent spirits as we set sail for America.

Chapter 44.

ABOARD THE TROOP SHIP MARINE TIGER ON THE CRUISE TO AMERICA

I decide to remain on deck. Before long, the Marine Tiger enters the beginning of the North Sea, and I find a place where I have a view of the disappearing land. I hear a plane droning overhead, and my thoughts immediately return to the Moltkefels in August of 1944, and our dangerous voyage on the Baltic Sea. However, as the plane continues its flight, I am quickly aware of the fact that there are no hostile bombers overhead, or submarines ahead, trying to target the Marine Tiger. With this comforting thought in mind, I return to the ship's hold, climb onto my bunk, and take a nap in the always-lighted room.

I am awakened in the late afternoon by the rocking of the ship. As I get out of my bunk, I feel a little dizzy. I walk onto the deck of the Marine Tiger, and I see that the waves have suddenly become higher, and the rocking of the ship has increased.

We are called to the large dining room at about five in the evening. Although the food is the best I have seen in years, with pieces of fried chickens, slices of beef, cooked potatoes, and bread, I have very little appetite. My mother and sister are sleeping in a different part of the ship, but we can eat together. Everyone else is able to eat a full meal. I hope that my ill feeling will pass and I can, once again, eat all this wonderful food provided by the American navy.

I go to my bunk early in the evening and fall asleep. I seem to have slept forever, because when I awaken, it is the following morning. The ship is rocking up and down, and I can hear waves smashing into the sides of the ship.

As I get up, I become violently ill, and have to run to the large bathroom to vomit. The only thing I can remember from the next couple of days, is my father giving me small amounts of water to drink—and vomiting. No one else in our family is seasick.

One morning, when I awaken, I finally feel well. The sickness caused by the never stopping rocking of the boat has gone, and I am able to eat a breakfast of eggs, fried potatoes, and ham, without feeling ill. I feel I have lost about four days of my life, but I am once again able to spend time on the open deck of the Marine Tiger. There are a lot of people on deck, either talking or simply staring into space at the waves—and more waves—in the distance. I am extremely grateful to join them.

On February 24, a group of Estonians gathers in a large room on the ship, and they celebrate the country's independence, which it gained shortly after the First World War. My mother has her visitor notebook with her, and she asks the other Estonians to sign it. There is no wine or beer, and the celebration is a quiet one as we remember our homeland and those left behind. I especially think of my beloved grandparents as we cruise toward America and our new life.

Two days later, we are told that we will be arriving in New York the morning of the following day. It has seemed, at least to me, to take forever to cross the stormy Atlantic in February. But at last, we will be arriving in our new country.

In anticipation, I go to bed early. After a restless sleep, we are awakened at 5:00 a.m. and given our final breakfast. We are instructed to gather in the large dining area and in the hallways with our belongings.

As soon as I leave my backpack with my parents and sister, I sneak on deck, instead of remaining in the dining room as we were told, and in the distance I see the lights of New York City. I am thrilled. I decide to throw my fur hat—which my mother makes me wear, and which I have always disliked—overboard. Then I return to my baggage—my absence, and that of my hat—unnoticed.

After a while, I sneak on deck again, and I see the Statue of Liberty, which I have seen pictures of in Geislingen. It is to our left, as the ship nears the harbor of New York, and it gets larger as we get closer. The sight of it makes me catch my breath. The Marine Tiger is nearly stopped, and I see two tugboats being stationed in the front and back of it. With relief, I fully realize that we have safely arrived in America.

I again go down below, and soon we are instructed to return to the deck and await instructions for departing the ship by way of the gangplank. As we stand in a line, prior to descending the gangplank, I see five men below who have already left the ship carrying large suitcases. They are being led away from the rest of the refugees. They are directed to go a short distance from the crowd, and as they stop, a man in a uniform directs them to open their five large suitcases.

When they have done this, I see them remove an accordion from each suitcase. There is a short discussion going on between the five and the man in uniform. The five strap the accordions onto their chests and begin to play. The sounds that emerge do not sound like a song, but like an earsplitting, screeching noise. I see them stop the movement of the accordions, place the instruments back in the cases, leave the cases on the ground, quickly gather their bags, and move on into the departing crowd.

My father tells me that the accordions were confiscated, because these immigrants from somewhere in Europe brought them along to be sold later, and this is illegal. Refugees are only allowed to bring in personal items, such as, clothing.

Shortly, it is our turn to descend, and we move along with the crowd in an orderly fashion. Our papers are checked once more, and before we know it, we are off the ship and onto the grounds of the Brooklyn Navy Yard, in New York City, USA.

Chapter 45.

FROM NEW YORK CITY TO FORT WORTH, TEXAS

It is crowded and clamorous as we stand with all our worldly belongings on February 27, 1949, wondering what to do next. My father tells us that on the day before the American immigration authorities gave him twelve American dollars. Three American dollars for each family member. Taxis begin to arrive. We hurriedly board one, with all of our belongings, and my father gives the driver a piece of paper with the name of the hotel where we are to meet Mr. Cozby.

The taxi speeds through the crowded streets. We are driving past tall buildings— unlike any we have seen. In Estonia and Germany, the buildings are only three or four stories high, and here they are reaching into the sky. We look, and point, and try to see everything as we speed along.

There are cars everywhere, and people walking— seemingly anywhere— at a rapid pace. The taxi starts and stops frequently to avoid hitting people, and keeps going quickly for at least a half hour, while horns are honking in the din, and we are looking out of the windows and trying to see everything. There are no bombed-out buildings. People do not look sad.

Finally, we arrive at our destination hotel. My father gives the driver a part of our twelve American dollars, and we stand with our belongings on the sidewalk in front of the hotel where we are to meet Mr. Cozby. I am surprised when we are met by an Estonian man who is standing in front of the hotel. My father knows him from before, and apparently, they had made plans to meet here at this time. They talk, and the Estonian tells us we should remain in New York, and we can live with his family. If Mr. Cozby does not arrive soon, I think this is a good plan.

However, my father explains he does not want to disappoint Mr. Cozby, because Mr. Cozby has offered to take our displaced family, and he is traveling a long distance to pick us up.

Just then, a man approaches us, calling out our family's name. He has dark hair and is shorter and heavier than my father. This must be Mr. Cozby. He is very friendly, laughing, shaking hands, and lifting my sister off the sidewalk, giving her a kiss on her cheek. Then a couple, a man and a woman, approach our group, and Mr. Cozby tells us these are his friends from Fort Worth. They have traveled along with Mr. Cozby from Texas, and they will be returning with us to Texas. We all exchange greetings. They are, also, laughing and friendly.

Just then, a driver brings Mr. Cozby's white car to the entrance of the hotel, and we are instructed to get into the small rear seat of what I learn is a two-door Chrysler Coupe. We place some of our luggage in the trunk, along with theirs, and when the seven of us are in the car, off we go with Mr. Cozby, driving through the streets of New York City.

The car is crowded, with Mr. Cozby and his friends in the front seat, and the four of us in the back with some of our luggage. My sister sits on my father's lap because there is not room for her on the seat. We are off to Texas without ever having entered even one building in New York City, USA.

As we pass through the city, we continue to be amazed at how tall the buildings are. I have never experienced—or expected—anything like this. It is like passing through a tunnel lined with moving people.

Mr. Cozby tells us that we will travel to the vicinity of Washington, DC, the capital of the United States. He also tells us that it will take about five hours to go the 250 miles from New York City to Washington, DC, but we will stop for the night before we reach the city, because he wants to drive into the city the following morning, and show us all the points of interest— such as, where the president of the country lives and the Capitol building, where the laws are made to run the country.

We keep driving, and do not mind our crowded back seat, because we feel so fortunate and excited to be in America. We are looking out the window all the time, and noticing that sometimes we go through villages and towns that look something like those in Estonia, especially, if they have some old buildings. But there are many more cars here—although, I do not see any that are Citroëns, like the car my father owned in Estonia.

We spend the night in what is called a motel, outside the city of Washington, DC, and I notice that Mr. Cozby pays for all our expenses during our journey. I think we are very lucky to have Mr. Cozby as our sponsor, because my father was given only three dollars for each of us and part of it he used to pay for the taxi. After eating a big, good-tasting supper—our first meal in America—we all go to our rooms and quickly go to sleep. We are exhausted from our cruise across the Atlantic Ocean and all we have seen today.

We are awakened early by Mr. Cozby, and after eating a large, wonderful breakfast with eggs and ham, all seven of us start the drive around Washington, DC. It is cloudy and raining, but we don't care. We never get out of the car. We are so high-spirited it doesn't matter how clearly we can see out of the car windows. The buildings we observe are in perfect condition, and this is something new to me, because since the war began, in all our travels, damage from bombs was everywhere.

After driving for about an hour throughout Washington, DC, Mr. Cozby tells us we will again resume the drive to our new home, which in his opinion will take at least three days, because it is approximately 1,300 miles. I notice Americans use miles, not kilometers, and I quickly try to calculate this.

As time passes, during this long drive, we try to talk to one another, but our English is limited, and Mr. Cozby and his friends do not speak German or Estonian. Mr. Cozby turns around sometimes to include us in the conversation, and I try to interpret for my parents.

It seems that every time Mr. Cozby stops for gasoline or a meal, and we get out of the car, it is a little warmer outside. Eventually, we no longer need our overcoats and hats, and we place them on our laps, along with our luggage.

One morning, we get started from our overnight stay, and after driving for a while we reach Fort Worth in Texas and arrive at Alf and Jessie's Barbeque Restaurant. It appears that Mr. and Mrs. Cozby own this restaurant, and she is named Jessie, and he is named Alf. I am wondering what a Barbeque is.

Chapter 46.

OUR LIFE IN TEXAS

We are suddenly surrounded by friendly Texans. They are greeting us, and everyone is talking at once. Mrs. Cozby is introduced to us, and she hugs my sister and lifts her up in the air. We did not expect this warm welcome. There are so many people. Shortly, we are invited inside the restaurant.

Whoever comes to shake our hands looks at my sister, and hugs her. Soon we are seated at a table, and Mr. Cozby tells us that we will be served a Texas meal called a Barbeque. The whole thing is a mystery to us, but once the food arrives, we are served meat with a brown sauce, along with bread, vegetable, and potatoes.

I have not seen such a large meal since leaving my grandparents' Tuule Farm in the fall of 1944. This meal tastes extremely good, and it convinces me that our days of hunger have ended.

After we finish all the food, Mr. and Mrs. Cozby drive us to their house nearby, and we enter. They tell us we will be staying with them a few days, and then we will be driven to the farm where we will live, near Springtown, a small town about twenty miles to the northwest of Fort Worth.

During these conversations, my sister and I continue our role as interpreters, and again, I realize our having studied English in Germany for four years is sufficient to make us understood and to make us able to include our parents in the conversations. Our parents are enthusiastic in trying to carry on conversations with these warm people, so we are very busy with trying to interpret.

The third day of our stay with the Cozbys, we are told by Mr. Cozby that we will make the move to the farm the next day because the house and the farm near Springtown are ready for our arrival.

Early the next day, we pack our belongings into Mr. Cozby's Chrysler and head for the farm. The farm is located about two miles outside Springtown, off a narrow gravel road. There is one other farm in the distance, but otherwise, the surroundings are remote, consisting mainly of fields. In this way, it is like the farms in Estonia, but without the forests. It is, also, much warmer here, and I notice that things are already growing. This warm weather is another surprise.

The house is a one-story wooden building, painted white, and as we follow Mr. Cozby inside, he asks us if we like it. My parents' reaction is favorable. My parents ask me to tell Mr. Cozby that it has been a long time since they have lived in a house of their own, and this house is wonderful, and they are very grateful to Mr. Cozby for all he has done for our family. This is not the first time they have thanked him—and I suspect we will thank him many times in the future.

Mr. Cozby then brings in a large box full of food items and tells us that he will return in two days and bring more food to last a week. Again, we thank him warmly.

The rooms are furnished. My parents will share a bedroom; my sister will have her own bedroom; and I will sleep on an enclosed porch. This is favorable with me, because I have never had my own room before.

The house is very clean, and we will not have to share the kitchen with other families. My mother is very pleased with it all. One of the rooms is almost filled with blankets, sheets, pillows, and towels, and there is even a radio in the living room. There is no phone, nor was there one at Tuule Farm, but there is electricity and a bathroom with a bathtub. There is also a refrigerator and an electric washing machine, neither of which we had in Viljandi, even though we had a maid. Again, my mother is well-pleased with all these American products.

After showing us everything, Mr. Cozby leaves, but promises to return as planned. My mother and father are beginning to arrange the rooms, and my sister and I decide to explore the outside. I remember Mr. Cozby having warned us about snakes in the uncut grass and in the weeds beyond the hard gravel yard surrounding the house. He had mentioned coral snakes, copperheads, rattle snakes, and bull snakes, and said that they are all poisonous, except for the bull snakes. I took careful note of what he said, because I do not remember any snakes in Estonia, but I am certain I do not want to come across these dangerous creatures here.

My sister and I follow Mr. Cozby's advice to stay out of the tall grass, and thankfully, we do not see any snakes. As we walk around, we discover a chicken coop and some trees in bloom. Maybe these are the peach trees that Mr. Cozby had mentioned. There are some short trees surrounding the fields, and a tall metal tower with propellers that go around in the wind. I remember Mr. Cozby told us that this is to pump the water to the house from the well. At Tuule Farm, we had to pump our water by hand, but this tall structure looks better and easier.

Then we see some people—a man, woman, and two girls—approaching from the direction of the nearby farm. As they arrive, the man introduces himself and his family. By now my parents have come outside, and I explain to them who our visitors are. They address me, and explain that if we need a ride to Springtown, we should let them know. I again interpret, and my mother asks me to invite them into the house, but they decline. They repeat their original offer of assistance, shake hands, and leave, waving to us as they return to their farm. We are relieved to have met such pleasant neighbors.

We continue to get settled as we await Mr. Cozby's return. In a few days, he arrives with several people and a truck pulling a trailer that holds a new Ford farm tractor and farming equipment. They unload, and tell my father how to operate the tractor because we did not have a tractor at the Tuule Farm. Mr. Cozby tells us the equipment is used to prepare the land for planting, and says he will return with the proper plants and seeds for vegetables and hay, which he calls Sudan grass. He says he will bring two horses to help with the farm work, plus fifty turkeys and young chickens, which will, also, become part of the operation. Pointing to a section of land towards the road, he instructs my father to prepare that area for growing tomatoes, melons, and other garden plants, which we can sell in Springtown.

My father seems to understand what is expected of us, even though we have never grown, or even seen, some of these plants, such as, melons. He indicates, through me, that he is happy to get started. After this, Mr. Cozby leaves with his friends.

Soon Mr. Cozby returns with all he promised—plus, food for the animals, and high leather boots for my father and me—to protect us from snake bites. Now we are ready to begin farming. My father decides to try out the horses for plowing near the road, and we are surprised that cars slow down and the occupants look as he is plowing with horses. He keeps at it all day, and then says he is going to use the new tractor, because it will be much faster than using horses as they did in Estonia.

About this time, a woman visits us. She says my sister and I will be enrolled at the Springtown High School, and we should find our school records from Germany. She will return in a few days, she adds, and further instruct us about starting school as soon as possible. I try to explain to her that I would rather work on the farm, helping my father, but she tells me I am expected to attend school, and due to my age, there are no exceptions. It looks like I cannot avoid this future boredom. Even in America.

As the woman is about to leave, my mother comes from the house with our school documents and hands them to the woman. I tell her the documents are in several languages, including English, and this seems to please her. As she prepares to leave, she tells us that she may return very soon, because after looking at the documents, she will be able to make the grade assignments and tell us when to start school.

Too soon for me, the woman returns. She tells us that my sister and I are ready to start school. Immediately.

She tells me I will be in the eleventh grade, as a junior, and my sister will be in the freshman, or ninth grade. I wonder to myself, again, how my sister can be only two years behind me, when I am three years older. I will be fifteen years old this month, and she will be twelve years old, just one week later.

The woman also says that on the following Monday, at 7:30 a.m., we will be picked up by a school bus at the end of our long driveway. After I explain all of this to my parents they seem to be overjoyed, and they warmly thank the lady. When she leaves, she says that she is looking forward to seeing us on Monday.

My sister is looking forward to school. Again, I wonder why. I would rather be driving the new tractor for my father, but my mother becomes very busy with getting our clothes ready for school. She even sings as she sews and mends and washes things.

The following Monday, my sister and I start school at Springtown High School, Springtown, Texas, USA. We walk to the end of our long driveway at 7:15 in the morning, and wait. A short while later, I see a yellow bus coming from our left, leaving a cloud of dust behind it. The bus stops, and the door opens. As we enter the bus, the driver waves and says, "Welcome." We answer in English.

When we begin to walk toward the back of the bus, I see a dozen smiling faces and students waving. I note that all the boys are dressed in white, short-sleeved, soft shirts, and blue pants rolled up at the bottom. I am wearing the formal, grey wool suit my mother made for me, and I vow to lose it soon.

As we sit down, I think perhaps the long road that began in August, 1944, has come to an end. And I have entered a friendly new world.

After a short ride, we arrive at the Springtown High School, and the woman who visited us on the farm to make arrangements for our attendance, meets us as we leave the bus. She takes me and my sister into the school office and gives us both class schedules, along with the list of subjects we will be taking for the remainder of the school year. She then escorts us to our assigned classrooms, where the school day will begin each morning.

She walks me to the front of the class, which happens to be Algebra, a subject with which I am much too familiar, and introduces me to the teacher. Then she leaves. I do not have a chance to choose a seat in the back row, farthest from the teacher, but I hope I will not be seen.

Here starts part of my new life, and it appears there is very little I can do to change it, even though I wish I could be working on the farm right now. I do not care for the attention I am getting from fellow students and teachers. They are friendly and smiling, but I would much rather fade into the group of students, as happened over the five years I attended school in Germany. The attention makes me uncomfortable, and I wish I could run out and return to Mr. Cozby's farm—or hide somewhere—but I don't know where. Everyone wants to know where Estonia is, and I try to explain it as well as I can.

As I am thinking of escape, a bell rings to announce the end of class. The teacher walks up to me and hands me my Algebra book and tells me which assignments I am to complete. He then walks me down the hall to the next class, introduces me to the teacher, and leaves.

This same process takes place throughout the day, as I am ushered from class to class and introduced, only to be interrupted by the lunch hour, which is spent in what is called a cafeteria. We are served a sandwich filled with ham, a glass of milk, and a piece of a sweet cake. Here, too, students greet me. I eat fast and try to keep my elbows stuck at my sides, as my mother insists. I do not see my sister. I hope she is at ease.

At the end of the first day, I have spent time in classes that are very similar to the classes I took in Germany, but I am aware that people are friendlier and happier here. I also spent time in what is called a study hall, where we can actually do assignments and ask the teacher in charge any questions we might have. I think this is so we will not have to spend so much time studying after school, as we did in Germany. I reflect briefly on all the hours my father and I spent studying mathematics after school, and I wonder if he will be waiting at the kitchen table when I arrive home. I will have plenty of books to show him, instead of the printed sheets of paper we used in war-torn Germany, where there were no books and most of our learning took place on the blackboard.

When school ends, close to 4:00 p.m., I am taken by the teacher outside where the busses are waiting. As I enter the bus, carrying an armload of books and notebooks, I see my sister near the front speaking to another girl who shares her seat. I can see she does not need me, so I do not greet her. I am happy she is making friends.

I walk to the middle of the bus, sit down next to a boy, and the bus leaves. He asks me if I liked school and I tell him that I did like my first day. What else can I say? I am relieved, however, that in about two-and-a-half months, the school year will be over and I will be working on Mr. Cozby's farm helping my father every day.

As we ride along, I think back to my school years in Germany, and I realize that I am getting much attention from other students and teachers, which was never the case before. Again, I wish that the attention would disappear, and I could somehow become part of the crowd. I wonder if it would help if I were shorter, because although no one mentions it in our family, I can see that I am much taller than most other boys in my classes. I wonder if I can droop down and go unnoticed.

When we arrive back at the farm, the driver tells my sister and me that he will see us tomorrow. As the bus pulls away, I look back, and see students waving to us. My sister and I wave back, and walk up the long road to the house where our parents are waiting.

We tell them about our first day in school and I say that I enjoyed it, which is somewhat a lie, because I would much rather have spent the day working on the farm. There is one thing that stays on my mind—my desire to look like the other boys and wear a white, short-sleeved, soft shirt, and blue pants rolled up at the bottom. I mention it to my parents, although, I know they have no money for this.

From here on, the school goes well. I get more used to the attention, and it seems that, at the end of each day, I can speak and understand more and more of the English language. This English speaking is a great satisfaction.

Somehow, my parents find the money to buy me a white short-sleeved soft shirt and blue pants for my birthday. I am very grateful to them. We learn the shirt is called a tee shirt, and the blue pants are called blue jeans. We pack the formal suit away. I still wear the shirts that my mother makes out of flour sacks, but no one says anything about them—or about the flour-sack dresses that my sister wears. Maybe they think these are a European custom, and maybe they are just being kind, but we are fortunate that our mother is a good seamstress. My sister says that all Estonian women are good at needlework, but our mother is especially good at it, and my sister is learning to be good at it, too.

In addition to the school days, when I return to the farm everyday, I help my father in the fields. I do enjoy this, because it reminds me of the Tuule Farm, and I think my father enjoys it, also. He grew up on a farm, before he entered Tartu University and studied economics, so he knows what he is doing. He seems happier and more relaxed now that we are away from war. He is working so hard that he seems too busy to question me about mathematics. Besides, I note that I am ahead in my mathematics because of the classes I had in Germany. This is a big, big relief. Sometimes, I do not mind, so much, the attention I receive from the teachers and students. They continue to be friendly, and both my sister and I are making friends.

One day, as we eat supper, my mother says she is fearful of the snakes that seem to be everywhere outside. My father and I understand her concern, because we see snakes every day in the field and attack them with our hoes. However, because we have high leather boots to protect us, we are not afraid. My mother adds that she is especially fearful of what are called scorpions, which at times appear in the bathtub.

She says that, a few days before, when she had killed a scorpion and shown it to Mr. Cozby, he had told her that they can bite and be very dangerous. Now these, in addition to the snakes, have become another new danger for her. My mother has never lived full-time on a farm, and these dangers are a great worry to her. In fact, before she married my father, she had a good position at a fine textile shop in Viljandi. After they were married, she never worked outside the house and she had a maid to help her in the house. So this farming is new to her. Even when she visited the Tuule Farm there were never poisonous snakes and scorpions. Now she says she intends to be especially careful when walking in the yard, and tells my sister, again, not to wander into the tall grass but to stay, instead, in the gravel yard which has no grass. She also cautions us to be careful if we are working in her vegetable garden. I think she and my sister need high leather boots. I wish we had the money to buy them each a pair.

Before the end of March, Mr. Cozby tells us that people from Parker County, where Springtown is located, are coming to the farm for a gathering, in order to welcome us to the community. This sounds pleasant to us and we look forward to meeting them. It is always good to know your neighbors, we feel.

When the day comes, we are amazed to see over sixty people arrive. They bring along gifts for the house and many food items, including jars of fruit and vegetables and five grown hens which they present to my mother. Someone even takes a photograph of her and tells us it will be in the newspaper.

Because the hens are old enough to lay eggs, my mind is at ease. Now, even if we are without food, we will be able to eat the eggs which the chickens will lay on a daily basis.

The visitors are very friendly, and as the day goes on, they all talk to us, which gives me a chance to interpret for my parents. We are laughing, and talking, and eating, and drinking Coca-Cola all afternoon. This time I do not drink the brown liquid too quickly.

Our visitors continue to tell us that, if we need anything, we should contact them. They also say we can expect some of them to arrive on Sunday morning and they will take us to a church in Springtown. Except for the occasional church service, Estonians have never been churchgoing people on a weekly basis, so this will be a new experience for us.

After the visitors leave and the dishes are put away, we gather in the kitchen and talk about the day. My parents are still amazed at having had such a wonderful experience and warm welcome. I tell them Mr. Cozby called it a housewarming, and they do such a gathering for every new family who moves to town. None of us has seen such a welcome for new families during our travels between D.P. camps. It is a great surprise for us after we have lived with war for so many years. I wonder if all Americans are as friendly as the people in Parker County.

I continue to become used to school, and unexpectedly, I actually like it. I think it is because of the friendliness surrounding me. Or maybe it's because the war is over, and we feel safe, or because we aren't eating watery soup, and rye bread that I must stuff in my pockets, or because we have our own bathroom, even though, it has occasional scorpions. We naturally remember our relatives who were left behind, and worry about them, and wish they could be here in safety. At the very least, we long to hear of them.

My sister and I make good friends, and this helps us to improve our English. As the days pass, some of the boys from school drive to the Cozby farm in the evenings, and they put sausages on a stick and cook them on an open fire. They refer to this as a wienie roast. I think these burned sausages are delicious food.

On most Saturday evenings, some neighbors stop in and give us a ride to Springtown to see a movie, or to simply walk around town and eat ice cream. This is something we have not done since leaving Estonia. There is no friendly Gasthaus, but I do not miss it. I have Coca-Cola.

True to their word, the good churchgoing people of Springtown drive out to pick us up for church on Sunday mornings. Most of our neighbors go to church, and we are pleased to be asked to go along with them—although, I am not always certain which church we are attending, because we go to one church with one family and then after the service that family hands us over to another family waiting for us in the church parking lot. The waiting family then takes us to their church service, and they sometimes hand us over to a third waiting family.

After a morning of this, we all take part in a huge meal that the women of one of the churches have prepared. I welcome this delicious food, because it is a good change from what we have at the farm—as we await the vegetables and fruit from my mother's garden.

Sometimes, after we are driven home on Sunday afternoon, we are again picked up and driven to an evening church service with an ice cream social afterward. Here I can eat as much ice cream as I want. I am very grateful for all this friendly attention.

However, this is the demanding growing season. Our crops were put in late because of our arrival time and my father and I feel, as time passes, that we should be spending these Sunday hours in the fields. I suggest hiding in the fields when Sunday mornings arrive, but my father will not even think of doing such a thing.

Fortunately, I think the church members see our difficulty—or maybe they themselves get so busy at this time of year, or maybe they feel they have done their part to welcome us to their churches, and now it is up to us. Anyway, the Sunday morning pickups become every other Sunday morning, and the churches become only one Baptist church. But I always look forward to the good food made by the friendly women—and all the ice cream I can eat.

One night, while my sister and I are still attending school, we are awakened by an alarming, howling noise. It sounds like a train passing nearby. My parents are already up, and they tell us to get dressed quickly. We hurry to leave the house and run after my father—without question—across the yard and into the cellar he knows about that is built into the hillside. It is pounding rain and howling wind, and we are soaking wet immediately.

As we enter, my father shines his flashlight toward the back of the cave-like cellar, and we see a huge brown snake on a shelf, curled around jars of canned vegetables. There seem to be more snakes on the other shelves. My mother screams, and her scream is followed by my sister starting to cry. We blindly back out of the cellar and run as fast as we can to the house. My mother and sister calm down, eventually, when we are in the house. After a time, the wind lets up, and we all go back to bed. But we are shaken by this new danger.

The next day at school, I learn from my classmates that this howling wind is called a tornado, and they get them here in the springtime. My friend explains to me that they look like a giant funnel, blowing wind and soil—and anything in their path—into the sky. He says one passed through the Springtown area last night and destroyed some of the buildings. I realize that we are very, very lucky to live a couple of miles from town.

Our family has never heard of a tornado, because we never saw one appear in Estonia or Germany. This experience reminds me of bombing raids in Germany during the war, except that when we entered a shelter during a raid in Germany, we did not see snakes. It seems there are many deadly dangers in this part of the world, also. This is something to think about.

One other day, when Mr. Cozby arrives bringing groceries, he asks me to go with him to a pond filled with clear water—a short distance beyond the cellar in the hill. He tells me he wants me to walk to this pond every day and see if there is any oil floating in the water. He tells me, if there is oil floating on top, it will mean there is oil below the surface. If I see oil, he can have it explored to find out if there is enough oil to make it worth paying for the price of drilling. He says, if there is enough oil, we will all be rich. He also says I should tell my father if I see oil and my father will know how to contact him.

I tell Mr. Cozby I will do as he asks. Later, I think about his request, and I decide my English must be improving because Mr. Cozby obviously thinks that I can understand him—and that I am capable of checking for oil. After this, every day after school, I hope to see oil floating on our pond. I reflect that with oil, we might have enough money to help our relatives in Estonia, or at least buy the farm from Mr. Cozby and stay here. Forever.

As time goes on, my parents make contact with a friend from Viljandi, who now resides with his family in the state of Wisconsin.

They exchange letters and learn more about other Estonian friends who have settled throughout the United States and Canada. These letters are a great comfort for them. It gives them a chance to hear from people who write their language and have experienced the same losses.

As we approach the middle of June, and my sister and I no longer go to school, we are pleased to see some of the crops begin to mature. Especially, the tomatoes. We begin to pick the ripened ones, and when Mr. Cozby comes, he takes these in baskets to Fort Worth where he sells them. Occasionally, he gives my father some money, and we use it to buy food items whenever we are given a ride to Springtown by a kind neighbor.

Sometimes, I drive the tractor to Springtown with the extra eggs we have gathered and I sell them to a grocer. This gives me an opportunity to see school friends and to eat an ice cream cone on the corner. I now feel I have become a part of the farm operation. Especially, because I am dressed in blue jeans and a white tee shirt, along with a wide-brimmed straw hat given to me by Mr. Cozby. I think I fit into this new world of America. I like it here.

We are told by Mr. Cozby that we can now release the young turkeys and young chickens from their coop because they are old enough to run free. The chickens still have to be fed, and they return to their coop at night, but the turkeys can perch outside and survive by eating the hoards of insects which are called grasshoppers. These insects are everywhere. We have not seen them before, because they do not exist in Estonia or Germany. At least, not in such huge numbers. However, compared to the war, these insects are nothing.

The heat has become intense, and at times, I feel I am going to faint. Estonia and Germany were never this hot. I fill a pail with cold water and carry it into the field where I work, mostly hoeing or picking tomatoes with my father. As we begin to feel the heat, we splash water onto our heads and faces or pour it over our heads. When the heat is unbearable, my mother and sister do not leave the house, except when the sun goes down. My father and I learn to remain indoors during the hottest part of the day and to sit in front of the two fans Mr. Cozby brought us. But compared to dead bodies and their stench, and the danger of bombs, this heat is nothing.

Well into July, Mr. Cozby says we can begin to pick the cantaloupes and watermelons. He shows us how to determine if they are ready for picking, by touching the surface and applying some pressure. If this outside is somewhat soft, the cantaloupes and watermelons are ready. As with the tomatoes, Mr. Cozby takes the cantaloupes and watermelons with him to Fort Worth to sell.

He tells us that we should start eating them, then shows us how they can be cut into slices and eaten. We do as he suggests, and we find them to be delicious. As I thought before—about eating the eggs from the five chickens—we have additional food in case we have no money to purchase any. I remind myself the milk from the cow my father milks every day gives us another valuable food, for just in case we are without funds.

During summer evenings, some of my friends from school come to the farm and we, again, eat wieners prepared on an open fire. They tell me they all belong to an organization called Future Farmers of America and encourage me to join. One day, the agriculture teacher arrives from Springtown High School and gives me a small card with my name on it below the letters FFA. He says that as soon as school starts again, he will see me and get me involved. This sounds wonderful to me, because I do like learning about farming. I know I want to have my own farm—someday.

As we enter August, Mr. Cozby arrives at the farm and asks all of us to gather around him in the yard. He looks very serious as he makes this request. I wonder why. He mainly speaks to me, and asks me to interpret for my parents. Quietly, he says he has decided to quit the farm operation—but we can stay and operate the farm for awhile. However, if we feel we do not wish to stay, we can leave, and he will make arrangements to make this possible. When we have decided, we should let him know. He does not linger, but says he will return soon. This is alarming news to us—and very unexpected. No wonder he looked so serious.

Immediately, after he leaves, we gather around the kitchen table and my parents start to discuss this serious and sudden change affecting our lives. We have had major changes and moves since August of 1944, and I reflect to myself that change almost seems normal to us. Nothing seems to be permanent—except change.

My mother begins our discussion by saying that she has always lived in cities, and although farm life has been a new experience, she would rather live without snakes, tornadoes, grasshoppers, scorpions, and heat. My father has enjoyed farming, but he says he still hopes he can use his banking knowledge in America when his English improves. My sister says she will go, if we do. I have loved this farm, which reminds me of my happy days at Tuule Farm, and I have been enjoying my life here, but I quickly see that we have no choice, because without Mr. Cozby's help we cannot survive. We must move on.

My father ends the discussion by saying he will immediately write a letter to his friend in Rockfield, Wisconsin, and find out if we can go there and find jobs and housing.

Somehow, we go on with our farm chores as though nothing has happened, and after a few days my parents receive a letter from their friend in Wisconsin. The letter tells us that when we arrive in Rockfield there will be work and housing available. This is very welcome news.

Soon Mr. Cozby visits us again, and we tell him of our decision and our plan. Mr. Cozby feels this is a wise decision and says he is relieved that we will have a place to go. Although he has never been to Wisconsin, he has heard of it. He has heard there are lots of farms in Wisconsin.

We mention our leaving to our neighbors, and explain it is because Mr. Cozby is giving up the farming operation. This news seems to quickly spread throughout Springtown and the surrounding area. People tell us that they will miss us, but they understand our situation. We assure them that we will miss them, too, and we will always remember their many kindnesses to us.

One day, one of the men from Springtown comes to the farm and gives my father some money, along with a paper. It says, "We the undersigned friends and neighbors of the Taagen family, realizing their need and to perpetrate a custom practiced among free people in a free Country, contribute according to our desire." Below the words are the signatures of many people and the amounts they contributed, from fifty cents to five dollars.

The visitor tells us that, although, the people hate to see us leave, they want to help us with expenses we will face when we leave Springtown. My parents are extremely grateful for this helpful gift, which amounts to almost forty dollars—and which is the most American money we have possessed. My mother cries, and my father shakes our visitor's hand more than once.

During his next visit, Mr. Cozby tells us he will return in a short while—which will be the end of August, a mere week away—and adds that we must be ready to leave when he appears. He also tells us arrangements have been made for someone to come and take all the animals the day we leave. This news about the animals makes me realize that our life on the farm is truly—over.

The week goes quickly as we hurriedly pack, and following my mother's orders, we leave the house spotless. On the date, Mr. Cozby arrives at noon. We have packed all our belongings in the two suitcases, the backpack, my mother's red case, my father's briefcase, and two extra bags which we have accumulated since our arrival. The two new bags are sturdy flour sacks.

We pack everything into Mr. Cozby's Chrysler, which we rode in from New York to Fort Worth. When we all climb into the car, Mr. Cozby tells my sister to sit next to him, with me on her right and with my parents in the back seat.

As we begin to drive down the long gravel path to the road to Springtown, I look at the fields. How sad it is to leave them. I look back, and my parents are both crying. Too soon, we are on the highway to Fort Worth.

I wonder if I will see this place again. Leaving Springtown seems very much like leaving Tallinn on the Moltkefels in August of 1944, because we are again carrying all our possessions with us—as we journey to an unknown place. However, I remind myself, there are no crying babies, and we are not wearing two layers of clothing, and there are no Russian prisoners, nor a one-legged accordion player, or bombs and torpedo threats. And we are all together.

When we arrive at the Fort Worth bus station, Mr. Cozby's wife, Jessie, is waiting for us. We all enter the station, and Mr. Cozby generously buys us tickets to Chicago and gives my father some extra money. We all shake hands and hug, and Mr. and Mrs. Cozby wish us luck. We wish them luck, also, and thank them—once again—for all their generosity—and for the friendship they have given to us, in addition to sponsoring our immigrant family, so we could come to this wonderful country.

They both leave. And we sit silently as we await the bus for Chicago. We are silent because of our thoughts, and because we know our accents will mark us as immigrants. When the bus arrives, it is half full. I am able to pick a seat next to a window, and my father sits next to me, and my mother and sister share a seat. We remain silent, as we wait for the bus to pull out of the station.

As we leave the city, darkness begins to fall. We are again traveling to a new destination. I make a mental note to learn more about this Wisconsin. I am glad they have farms there. In the meantime, I content myself by looking out at America from the window of the bus. I quietly practice English, particularly my pronunciation of Tuesday, with a double "u" sound, as in Tuule, so nobody in Wisconsin will suspect I am an immigrant. Especially, I think, they will not suspect my background when I am wearing my blue jeans and white tee shirt. Until my pronunciation is perfect, however, I will be obliged to say, "We are leaving Springtown, Texas, for Rockfield, Wisconsin, on the day after Monday—or the day before Wednesday— in August, 1949." And we will survive, once again. We are displaced—but not lost.

EPILOGUE

The Taagen family arrived safely in Rockfield, Wisconsin, in August, 1949, where they immediately found employment at the Rockfield Canning Company and housing at the local boarding house with the other itinerant clientele.

Very soon, Mr. A. J. Klumb, the owner of the canning company, generously built a small house for them, which Tony's and Linda's parents, Ludmilla and Johannes, paid for over the years.

Tõnu, who was quickly called Tony by Americans, and Linda, attended high school in nearby West Bend, Wisconsin, where they became well-adjusted American teenagers. They worked at the canning company and at other jobs—during summers and school vacations—to help the family and to pay for their college educations.

Tony lost his Estonian accent, with the exception of his pronunciation of the word Tuesday, the day after Monday. When he entered Marquette University in Milwaukee, Wisconsin, approximately three years after arriving in America, his classmates were unable to detect his background through his speech or outward appearance, and he felt no need to enlighten them, because he wanted to be accepted as an American. He recounts the story of buying a beer in a Madison, Wisconsin, hotel after a football game between Marquette University and the University of Wisconsin-Madison: He was approached by a gentleman who pointed to him and said to his wife, "Now there is a real all-American young man." Tony—tall, blond, tanned, wearing his blue jeans and white tee shirt— felt this remark signaled his legitimacy as an American.

After five years in America, the Taagen family was sworn in as US citizens and Tõnu officially became Tony.

He was able to avoid becoming a banker, much to his father's disappointment, but instead enjoyed a career in the Wisconsin Department of Corrections after serving with the United States Army in Germany and in France. Thanks to the GI Bill, he was able to finance school, once again, and received his Master of Science in Social Work from the University of Wisconsin-Milwaukee, while helping his American-born wife raise their six mischievous sons—who were not unlike him.

Linda, meanwhile, grew into a beautiful young woman and continued to be an exemplary student, differing markedly from her brother. She graduated from the renowned Milwaukee Downer College in Milwaukee, Wisconsin, with a degree in home economics. She raised two lovely daughters and a handsome son with her American-born husband and eventually established a superior home accessories store, *The Past Basket*, which she continues to successfully operate with her peerless European-American style in Geneva, Illinois, and in Milwaukee, Wisconsin.

Both have returned to Estonia several times since the restoration of Estonian independence in 1991, to show their brave, charming homeland to their spouses, children, and grandchildren—and to visit their dearly loved, surviving relatives.

Unfortunately, their parents, Johannes and Ludmilla, were unable to return to their beloved Estonia before they died. Like many displaced persons, their hearts remained in their homeland, and they never truly Americanized. Johannes, because of the language barrier, did not find employment as a banker. However, he became the manager of the warehouse for the Rockfield Canning Company. Ludmilla, after employment cleaning houses, became an assembly worker at Doerr Electric in Cedarburg, Wisconsin. Her superb needlework, which she learned as a young woman in Estonia, has become her legacy.

Through frugality, this immigrant couple was able to buy a lakefront property in Manitowish Waters, Wisconsin, which reminded them of their Estonian landscape. Here Johannes built a beautiful cottage. Like other displaced persons, this heroic couple, who saved themselves and their children from tyranny, never ceased in their efforts to contact their lost relatives and friends who were left behind. As often as possible, they sent them letters and packages of food and clothing in an attempt to make their lives easier under Russian occupation.

However, letters from Estonia were often censored—words were blacked out or cut out. It is supposed that Tony's beloved grandparents from Tuule Farm, Mihkel and Mari, lived on a collective farm during the Russian occupation. In her later years, Mari, who lived to be ninety-four, was looked after by surviving relatives. Somehow, this caring woman was able to knit and send pairs of Estonian-patterned, lovely baby booties and baby mittens to Tony's and Linda's children, her great-grandchildren in America. Linda remembers that this self-sufficient woman could knit a pattern while sitting in the dark, from wool that she had sheared, spun, and dyed, before she knitted it with fine stitches upon tiny needles. These treasured gifts grace the Taagen Xmas tree each year. Mihkel, who was eleven years older than his wife Mari, died at eighty-three, the year after the Taagen family immigrated to America.

Their son, Alfred Tagen, (Johannes's brother and Tony's and Linda's uncle) along with his wife Marta and daughter Hille, was sent to Siberia in 1941. He was executed by the Soviets, probably as a major, on April 1, 1942 in Sevurallag prison camp, Sosva, Siberia. Hille was able to return to Estonia—after fourteen years— in 1955, to begin study at the University of Tartu and eventually became a surgeon. One year later, in 1956, Marta was allowed to return to Estonia. Uno—Hille's and Valdo's brother and Marta's and Alfred's son—also became a physician but is now deceased. Therefore, Hille is the only living relative who knew Tony and Linda as children in Estonia. They have remained close to her and her family and are deeply pleased that their children and grandchildren are continuing friendships with their Estonians cousins.

Christmas remained, for Johannes and Ludmilla, a sad time of remembrance, and New Year's Eve, a time for hope. The birth of each grandchild brought tears of joy, along with admonishments from both of them to always do your best—especially in school—"because they cannot take your education away from you."

Tony and Linda, as did their parents, remain ever grateful to the United States of America for liberating them.

Tony has written this true account of his interrupted boyhood in response to the curiosity of his adult children and because he wants them to have the correct facts regarding why his pointer finger is crooked. Now he can return to being that "all-American (not so young) man" and live in the present, looking ahead, not back, and anticipating— among other enjoyments—The Yellow Bus Reunion—a summer gathering of former high school classmates who accepted Tony and Linda so generously into this place of refuge, after their five-year journey into the unknown.

Linda Taagen McFadden gracefully resides in Geneva, Illinois, and still puts up with her older brother.

Tony M. Taagen abides in Mequon, Wisconsin, along with the two large suitcases, their mother's small red suitcase, their father's briefcase, the grey plaid blanket woven by their grandmother at Tuule Farm, his wife Connie, and his Maine Coon cat Hemingway.

SIGNIFICANT DATES

1867–1950	Mihkel Tagen
1878–1972	Mari Kallion Tagen
1879–1952	Kaarel Rand
1883–1965	Lina Koesel Rand
1905–1978	Johannes Taagen (Tagen)
1908–2003	Ludmilla Rand Taagen
March 16, 1934-	Tõnu (Tony) Taagen
March 23, 1937-	Linda Taagen McFadden

August 23, 1939 Molotov-Ribbentrop Pact. Germany gives Russia the right to occupy Baltic Countries.

September, 1939–September, 1941

Russia occupies Estonia.

Johannes Taagen is in hiding during this time; however, the children are simply told that he is away. Adults do not tell children what is happening. Schools are open, and for children, life continues as before the occupation.

September 24, 1939 Russia establishes military bases in the Baltics.

October, 1939 — Russian troops enter Estonia.

June, 1940 — Russia occupies all of Estonia.

June 14, 1941 — Russians begin to deport Estonians to Siberia.

June 21, 1941 — German army attacks Russia, and by June 23, is well into Lithuania as it advances toward Latvia and Estonia. Although Germany has attacked, there is a continued Russian presence and danger during June–September, 1941.

June 22, 1941 — Johannes remains in hiding. There is a knock on the door in Viljandi and a warning that the Russians are coming. Ludmilla, Tõnu, and Linda escape out the back door of their house and walk through the night to Tuule Farm. The next day, Ludmilla leaves the farm and goes to Tallinn where she digs ditches for the Russian army. It is not known whether Johannes and Lumilla see one another during this time because he is in hiding and her living arrangements are unknown.

August 28, 1941 — Russians leave Tallinn, and Germans take over until September, 1944.

September, 1941–September, 1944

During the German occupation life is normal, and Johannes returns to his job as President of the Estonian Farmers' Society Bank and is able to maintain his interests in the Sakala newspaper in Viljandi.

August, 1944 — It is feared that the Russians will soon return. Ludmilla, Tõnu, and Linda leave Tuule Farm, travel to Piirita, and board the Moltkefels freighter

	in Tallinn to escape to Germany. Johannes makes an appearance to bid them farewell but must remain in the country because no males over age sixteen are allowed to leave the country. He expects to join the German army.
September, 1944	Exact date is unknown, but Johannes escapes from Tallinn and boards a ship bound for Germany, just before the Russian army retakes Tallinn. There is already fighting in the streets when he leaves.
1944–1949	Taagen family lives in Germany at a farm in Graitschen and later in displaced persons camps.

Significant Dates During This Period In Germany:

Early 1945	Death of Valdo.
February 13, 1945	Bombing of Dresden by Allies.
April 13, 1945	Americans liberate Graitschen on Ludmilla's thirty-seventh birthday.
October, 1946	Tõnu's eye injury in Wiesbaden.
June,1948–May,1949	Berlin Blockade.
1945–1949	Displaced persons (DP) camps in chronological order: Jena, Wiesbaden, Kassel, Geislingen an der Steige.

Significant Dates After Germany:

February, 1949	The Taagen family leaves Germany on the Marine Tiger from Bremerhaven in northern Germany, bound for the Brooklyn Navy Yard, New York City, New York.

February 27, 1949	The family arrives in New York City.
March–August, 1949	The family lives in Springtown, Texas.
August, 1949	Taagen family arrives in Rockfield, Wisconsin.
November 11, 1954	The Taagen family become citizens of the United States of America at the Federal Building in Milwaukee, Wisconsin.
1952–1956	Tony Taagen attends Marquette University, Milwaukee, Wisconsin, and graduates with a BS in business administration.
1957–1959	Tony Taagen serves in the United States Army, stationed in Germany and France, attached to the 801st Engineer Battalion.
May 28, 1972	Tony Taagen receives an MS in Social Work from the University of Wisconsin-Milwaukee.
August 20, 1991	Estonian Reindependence. A national holiday in Estonia.

ACKNOWLEDGMENTS

First of all, my eternal gratitude goes to my parents, Johannes and Ludmilla Taagen. Their bravery and foresight, and that of all my Estonian relatives, astounds and humbles me to this day.

Everlasting thankfulness also to my sister, Linda Taagen McFadden, for being there then—and now.

In addition, I am forever grateful to my wife, Connie, for not allowing me to procrastinate any longer and for being my unyielding editor. I know it was tough, in the extreme, to keep me on task.

I sincerely thank my six sons, who continually asked me, "Isn't the book finished yet?" Thank you, Tom, I never knew what a flash drive was before you acquainted me with it. I treasure your comprehensive reading of the book and your insightful comments. It was amazing to hear that you have kept my US Army-issue loden green high-tops from my YMCA camping days in Geislingen.

A fervent thank you is owed to my lovely daughters-in-law, Jessica Taagen and Deborah Taagen, who provided invaluable computer expertise along with selfless patience. All would have been lost, not merely displaced, without you. Also, to Maureen McFadden Olofsson, my talented professional photographer niece, who did the same and then saved me by putting the illustrations on JPEG. (I remain ignorant as to what JPEG means.)

Peg Noonan, Linda Taagen, and Patty Taagen, my other charming daughters-in-law, have given me encouragement when I most needed it. Thank you, forever, for your unstinting support. Peg, your literary discernment has been invaluable. Not only were you the first to read this book, but you reassured my anxious soul.

Hiie Olvet Laugesaar, your contact over the years has meant the world—an inspiration for this book—from your first brave visit in 1992—to now. Hille Tagen Olvet, you remain my unbreakable link to our homeland.

Undying gratitude to my incomparable friend, Dorothy Dey, who has always been there when I need her. (Yes, Dee, I will get this copy-righted tomorrow.) I am also indebted to my superior friend, Jane Brite, for her matchless enthusiasm and knowledge regarding publishing. I trust my story does not disappoint.

And finally, thank you to all my friends and relatives—and know this includes you: David McFadden, Heather McFadden Redic, and Dan McFadden—who encouraged me along the way. I hope your faith in me has been well placed. If this book interests you, and others, the long journey has been worthwhile.

ABOUT THE AUTHOR

Tony Michael Taagen was born in Viljandi, Estonia, but found his muse in the Village of Belleville, Dane County, Wisconsin, as he contemplated life from the verandas of his wife's old family home. When they reluctantly left this picturesque village after five creative years, he received a treasured certificate of appreciation from the Village President in recognition of his service as the "Official Pooper Scooper" of dung dropped by Amish horses pulling carriages that were often parked in the alley next to the stately abode.

He now abides in Mequon, Wisconsin, along with the two large suitcases, his mother's small red suitcase, his father's briefcase, the grey plaid blanket woven by his grandmother at Tuule Farm—all featured in this memoir—his wife Connie, and his Maine Coon cat Hemingway. Tony is passively-aggressively writing another memoir about his service in the United States Army—tentatively titled—"Paid Vacation."

Made in the USA
Lexington, KY
17 November 2013